How to Overcome Sin and Temptation

By John Owen

Printed in the USA

Table of Contents

To the Reader

Christian Reader,

If thou art in any measure awake in these days wherein we live, and hast taken notice of the manifold, great, and various temptations wherewith all sorts of persons that know the Lord and profess his name are beset, and whereunto they are continually exposed, with what success those temptations have obtained, to the unspeakable scandal of the gospel, with the wounding and ruin of innumerable souls, I suppose thou wilt not inquire any farther after other reasons of the publishing of the ensuing warnings and directions, being suited to the times that pass over us, and thine own concernment in them. This I shall only say to those who think meet to persist in any such inquiry, that though my first engagement for the exposing of these meditations unto public view did arise from the desires of some, whose avouching the interest of Christ in the world by personal holiness and constant adhering to every thing that is made precious by its relation to him, have given them power over me to require at any time services of greater importance; yet I dare not lay my doing of it so upon that account, as in the least to intimate that, with respect to the general state of things mentioned, I did not myself esteem it seasonable and necessary. The variety of outward providences and dispensations wherewith I have myself been exercised in this world, with the inward trials they have been attended withal, added to the observation that I have had advantages to make of the ways and walkings of others,—their beginnings, progresses, and endings, their risings and falls, in profession and conversation, in darkness and light,—have left such a constant sense and impression of the power and danger of temptations upon my mind and spirit, that, without other pleas and pretences, I cannot but own a serious call unto men to beware, with a discovery of some of the most eminent ways and means of the prevalency of present temptations, to have been, in my own judgement, in this season needful.

But now, reader, if thou art amongst them, who takest no notice of these things, or carest not for them,—who hast no sense of the efficacy and dangers of temptations in thine own walking and profession, nor hast observed the power of them upon others,—who discernest not the manifold advantages that they have got in these days, wherein all things are shaken, nor hast been troubled or moved for the sad successes they have had amongst professors; but supposest that all things are well within doors and without, and would be better couldst thou obtain fuller satisfaction to some of thy lusts in the pleasures or profits of the world,—I desire thee to know that I write not for thee, nor do esteem thee a fit reader or judge of what is here written. Whilst all the issues of providential dispensations, in reference to the public concernments of these nations, are perplexed and entangled, the footsteps of God lying in the deep, where his paths are not known; whilst, in particular, unparalleled distresses and strange prosperities are measured out to men, yea, to professors; whilst a spirit of error, giddiness, and delusion goes forth with such strength and efficacy, as it seems to have received a commission to go and prosper; whilst there are such divisions, strifes, emulations, attended with such evil surmises, wrath, and revenge, found amongst brethren; whilst the desperate issues and products of men's temptations are seen daily in partial and total apostasy, in the decay of love, the overthrow of faith, our days being filled with fearful examples of backsliding, such as former ages never knew; whilst there is a visible declension from reformation seizing upon the professing party of these nations, both as to personal holiness and zeal for the interest of Christ;—he that understands not that there is an "hour of temptation" come upon the world, to "try them that dwell upon the earth," is doubtless either himself at present captivated under the power of some woful lust, corruption, or temptation, or is indeed stark blind, and knows not at all what it is to serve God in temptations. With such, then, I have not at present to do. For those who have in general a sense of these things,—who also, in some measure are able to consider that the plague is begun, that they may be farther awakened to look about them, lest the infection have approached nearer to them, by some secret and imperceptible ways, than they did apprehend; or lest they should be surprised at unawares hereafter by any of those temptations that in these days either waste at noon or else walk in darkness,—is the ensuing warning intended. And for the sake of them that mourn in secret for all the abominations that are found among and upon them that profess the gospel, and who are under the conduct of the Captain of their salvation, fighting and resisting the power of temptations, from what spring soever they rise in themselves, are the ensuing directions proposed to consideration.

That our faithful and merciful High Priest, who both suffered and was tempted, and is on that account touched with the feeling of our infirmities, would accompany this small discourse with seasonable supplies of his Spirit and suitable mercy to them that shall consider it, that it may be useful to his servants for the ends whereunto it is designed, is the prayer of him who received this handful of seed from his storehouse and treasure.

John Owen.

Chapter 1

"Watch and pray, that ye enter not into temptation."—Matt. xxvi. 41

These words of our Saviour are repeated with very little alteration in three evangelists; only, whereas Matthew and Mark have recorded them as above written, Luke reporteth them thus: "Rise and pray, lest ye enter into temptation;" so that the whole of his caution seems to have been, "Arise, watch and pray, that ye enter not into temptation."

Solomon tells us of some that "lie down on the top of a mast in the midst of the sea," Prov. xxiii. 34,—men overborne by security in the mouth of destruction. If ever poor souls lay down on the top of a mast in the midst of the sea, these disciples with our Saviour in the garden did so. Their Master, at a little distance from them, was "offering up prayers and supplications, with strong crying and tears," Heb. v. 7, being then taking into his hand and beginning to [1] taste that cup that was filled with the curse and wrath due to their sins;—the Jews, armed for his and their destruction, being but a little more distant from them, on the other hand. Our Saviour had a little before informed them that that night he should be betrayed, and be delivered up to be slain; they saw that he was "sorrowful, and very heavy," Matt. xxvi. 37; nay, he told them plainly that his "soul was exceeding sorrowful, even unto death," verse 38, and therefore entreated them to tarry and watch with him, now he was dying, and that for them. In this condition, leaving them but a little space, like men forsaken of all love towards him or care of themselves, they fall fast asleep! Even the best of saints, being left to themselves, will quickly appear to be less than men,—to be nothing. All our own strength is weakness, and all our wisdom folly. Peter being one of them,—who but a little before had with so much self-confidence affirmed that though all men forsook him, yet he never would so do,—our Saviour expostulates the matter in particular with him: verse 40, "He saith unto Peter, Could you not watch with me one hour?" as if he should have said, "Art thou he, Peter, who but now boastedst of thy resolution never to forsake me? Is it likely that thou shouldst hold out therein, when thou canst not watch with me one hour? Is this thy dying for me, to be dead in security, when I am dying for thee?" And indeed it would be an amazing thing to consider that Peter should make so high a promise, and be immediately so careless and remiss in the pursuit of it, but that we find the root of the same treachery abiding and working in our own hearts, and do see the fruit of it brought forth every day, the most noble engagements unto obedience quickly ending in deplorable negligence, Rom. vii. 18.

In this estate our Saviour admonishes them of their condition, their weakness, their danger, and stirs them up to a prevention of that ruin which lay at the door: saith he, "Arise, watch and pray."

I shall not insist on the particular aimed at here by our Saviour, in this caution to them that were then present with him; the great temptation that was coming on them, from the scandal of the cross, was doubtless in his eye;—but I shall consider the words as containing a general direction to all the disciples of Christ, in their following of him throughout all generations.

There are three things in the words:—

I. The evil cautioned against,—temptation.
II. The means of its prevalency,—by our entering into it.
III. The way of preventing it,—watch and pray.

It is not in my thoughts to handle the common-place of temptations, but only the danger of them in general, with the means of preventing that danger; yet, that we may know what we affirm, and whereof we speak, some concernments of the general nature of temptation may be premised.

I. First, For the general nature of tempting and temptation, it lies among things indifferent; to try, to experiment, to prove, to pierce a vessel, that the liquor that is in it may be known, is as much as is signified by it. Hence God is said sometime to tempt; and we are commanded as our duty to tempt, or try, or search ourselves, to know what is in us, and to pray that God would do so also. So temptation is like a knife, that may either cut the meat or the throat of a man; it may be his food or his poison, his exercise or his destruction.

Secondly, Temptation in its special nature, as it denotes any evil, is considered either actively, as it leads to evil, or passively, as it hath an evil and suffering in it: so temptation is taken for affliction, James i. 2; for in that sense, we are to "count it all joy when we fall into temptation;" in the other, that we "enter not into it."

Again, actively considered, it either denotes in the tempter a design for the bringing about of the special end of temptation, namely, a leading into evil; so it is said, that "God tempts no man," James i. 13, with a design for sin as such;—or the general nature and end of temptation, which is trial; so "God tempted Abraham," Gen. xxii. 1. And he proveth or tempteth by false prophets, Deut. xiii. 3.

Now, as to God's tempting of any, two things are to be considered:—1. The end why he doth it; 2. The way whereby he doth it.

For the first, his general ends are two:—

(1.) He doth it to show unto man what is in him,—that is, the man himself; and that either as to his grace or to his corruption. (I speak not now of it as it may have a place and bear a part in judiciary obduration.) Grace and corruption lie deep in the heart; men oftentimes deceive themselves in the search after the one or the other of them. When we give vent to the soul, to try what grace is there, corruption comes out; and when we search for corruption, grace appears. So is the soul kept in uncertainty; we fail in our trials. God comes with a gauge that goes to the bottom. He sends his instruments of trial into the bowels and the inmost parts of the soul, and lets man see what is in him, of what metal he is constituted. Thus he tempted

Abraham to show him his faith. Abraham knew not what faith he had (I mean, what power and vigour was in his faith) until God drew it out by that great trial and temptation. [2] When God says he knew it, he made Abraham to know it. So he tried Hezekiah to discover his pride; God left him that he might see what was in his heart, 2 Chron. xxxii. 31. He knew not that he had such a proud heart, so apt to be lifted up, as he appeared to have, until God tried him, and so let out his filth, and poured it out before his face. The issues of such discoveries to the saints, in thankfulness, humiliation, and treasuring up of experiences, I shall not treat of.

(2.) God doth it to show himself unto man, and that,—

1. In a way of preventing grace. A man shall see that it is God alone who keeps from all sin. Until we are tempted, we think we live on our own strength. Though all men do this or that, we will not. When the trial comes, we quickly see whence is our preservation, by standing or falling. So was it in the case of Abimelech, Gen. xx. 6, "I withheld thee."

2. In a way of renewing grace. He would have the temptation continue with St Paul, that he might reveal himself to him in the sufficiency of his renewing grace, 2 Cor. xii. 9. We know not the power and strength that God puts forth in our behalf, nor what is the sufficiency of his grace, until, comparing the temptation with our own weakness, it appears unto us. The efficacy of an antidote is found when poison hath been taken; and the preciousness of medicines is made known by diseases. We shall never know what strength there is in grace if we know not what strength there is in temptation. We must be tried, that we may be made sensible of being preserved. And many other good and gracious ends he hath, which he accomplisheth towards his saints by his trials and temptations, not now to be insisted on.

2. For the ways whereby God accomplisheth this his search, trial or temptation, these are some of them:—

(1.) He puts men on great duties, such as they cannot apprehend that they have any strength for, nor indeed have. So he tempted Abraham by calling him to that duty of sacrificing his son;—a thing absurd to reason, bitter to nature, and grievous to him on all accounts whatever. Many men know not what is in them, or rather what is ready for them, until they are put upon what seems utterly above their strength; indeed, upon what is really above their strength. The duties that God, in an ordinary way, requires at our hands are not proportioned to what strength we have in ourselves, but to what help and relief is laid up for us in Christ; and we are to address ourselves to the greatest performances with a settled persuasion that we have not ability for the least. This is the law of grace; but yet, when any duty is required that is extraordinary, that is a secret not often discovered. In the yoke of Christ it is a trial, a temptation.

(2.) By putting them upon great sufferings. How many have unexpectedly found strength to die at a stake, to endure tortures for Christ! yet their call to it was a trial. This, Peter tells us, is one way whereby we are brought into trying temptations, 1 Pet. i. 6, 7. Our temptations arise from the "fiery trial;" and yet the end is but a trial of our faith.

(3.) By his providential disposing of things so as that occasions unto sin will be administered unto men, which is the case mentioned, Deut. xiii. 3; and innumerable other instances may be adjoined.

Now, they are not properly the temptations of God, as coming from him, with his end upon them, that are here intended; and therefore I shall set these apart from our present consideration. It is, then, temptation in its special nature, as it denotes an active efficiency towards sinning (as it is managed with evil unto evil) that I intend.

In this sense temptation may proceed either singly from Satan, or the world, or other men in the world, or from ourselves, or jointly from all or some of them, in their several combinations:—

(1.) Satan tempts sometimes singly by himself, without taking advantage from the world, the things or persons of it, or ourselves. So he deals in his injection of evil and blasphemous thoughts of God into the hearts of the saints; which is his own work alone, without any advantage from the world or our own hearts: for nature will contribute nothing thereunto, nor any thing that is in the world, nor any man of the world; for none can conceive a God and conceive evil of him. Herein Satan is alone in the sin, and shall be so in the punishment. These fiery darts are prepared in the forge of his own malice, and shall, with all their venom and poison, be turned into his own heart for ever.

(2.) Sometimes he makes use of the world, and joins forces against us, without any helps from within. So he tempted our Saviour, by "showing him all the kingdoms of the world, and the glory of them." [3] And the variety of the assistances he finds from the world, in persons and things which I must not insist on,—the innumerable instruments and weapons he takes from thence of all sorts and at all seasons,—are inexpressible.

(3.) Sometimes he takes in assistance from ourselves also. It is not with us as it was with Christ when Satan came to tempt him. He declares that he "had nothing in him," John xiv. 30. It is otherwise with us: he hath, for the compassing of most of his ends, a sure party within our own breasts, James i. 14, 15. Thus he tempted Judas: he was at work himself; he put it into his heart to betray Christ; Luke xxii. 3, "he entered into him" for that purpose. And he sets the world at work, the things of it, providing for him "thirty pieces of silver" (verse 5, "They covenanted to give him money"); and the men of it, even the priests and the Pharisees; and calleth in the assistance of his own corruption,—he was covetous, "a thief, and had the bag."

I might also show how the world and our own corruptions do act single by themselves, and jointly in conjunction with Satan and one another, in this business of temptation. But the truth is, the principles, ways, and means of temptations, the kinds, degrees, efficacy, and causes of them, are so inexpressibly large and various; the circumstances of them, from providence, natures, conditions, spiritual and natural, with the particular cases thence arising, so innumerable and impossible to be comprised within any bound or order, that to attempt the giving an account of them would be to undertake that which would be endless. I shall content myself to give a description of the general nature of that which we are to watch against; which will make way for what I aim at.

Temptation, then, in general, is any thing, state, way, or condition that, upon any account whatever, hath a force or efficacy to seduce, to draw the mind and heart of a man from its obedience, which God requires of him, into any sin, in any degree of it whatever.

In particular, that is a temptation to any man which causes or occasions him to sin, or in any thing to go off from his duty, either by bringing evil into his heart, or drawing out that evil that is in his heart, or any other way diverting him from communion with God, and that constant, equal, universal obedience, in matter and manner, that is required of him.

For the clearing of this description I shall only observe, that though temptation seems to be of a more active importance, and so to denote only the power of seduction to sin itself, yet in the Scripture it is commonly taken in a neuter sense, and denotes the matter of the temptation or the thing whereby we are tempted. And this is a ground of the description I have given of it. Be it what it will, that from any thing whatever, within us or without us, hath advantage to hinder in duty, or to provoke unto or in any way to occasion sin, that is a temptation, and so to be looked on. Be it business, employment, course of life, company, affections, nature, or corrupt design, relations, delights, name, reputation, esteem, abilities, parts or excellencies of body or mind, place, dignity, art,—so far as they further or occasion the promotion of the ends before mentioned, they are all of them no less truly temptations that the most violent solicitations of Satan or allurements of the world, and that soul lies at the brink of ruin who discerns it not. And this will be farther discovered in our process.

Chapter 2

II. Having showed what temptation is, I come, secondly, to manifest what it is to enter into temptation.

1. This is not merely to be tempted. It is impossible that we should be so freed from temptation as not to be at all tempted. Whilst Satan continues in his power and malice, whilst the world and lust are in being, we shall be tempted. "Christ," says one, "was made like unto us, that he might be tempted; and we are tempted that we may be made like unto Christ." Temptation in general is comprehensive of our whole warfare; as our Saviour calls the time of his ministry the time of his "temptations," Luke xxii. 28. We have no promise that we shall not be tempted at all; nor are to pray for an absolute freedom from temptations, because we have no such promise of being heard therein. The direction we have for our prayers is, "Lead us not into temptation," Matt. vi. 13; it is "entering into temptation" that we are to pray against. We may be tempted, yet not enter into temptation. So that,—

2. Something more is intended by this expression than the ordinary work of Satan and our own lusts, which will be sure to tempt us every day. There is something signal in this entering into temptation, that is not the saints' every day's work. It is something that befalls them peculiarly in reference to seduction unto sin, on one account or other, by the way of allurement or affrightment.

3. It is not to be conquered by a temptation, to fall down under it, to commit the sin or evil that we are tempted to, or to omit the duties that are opposed. A man may "enter into temptation," and yet not fall under temptation. God can make a way for a man to escape; when he

is in, he can break the snare, tread down Satan, and make the soul more than a conqueror, though it have entered into temptation. Christ entered into it, but was not in the least foiled by it. But,—

4. It is, as the apostle expresseth it, 1 Tim. vi. 9, empiptein,"to fall into temptation," as a man falls into a pit or deep place where are gins or snares, wherewith he is entangled; the man is not presently killed and destroyed, but he is entangled and detained,—he knows not how to get free or be at liberty. So it is expressed again to the same purpose, 1 Cor. x. 13, "No temptation hath taken you;" that is, to be taken by a temptation and to be tangled with it, held in its cords, not finding at present a way to escape. Thence saith Peter, 2 Epist. ii. 9, "The Lord knoweth how to deliver the godly out of temptations." They are entangled with them; God knows how to deliver them out of them. When we suffer a temptation to enter into us, then we "enter into temptation." Whilst it knocks at the door we are at liberty; but when any temptation comes in and parleys with the heart, reasons with the mind, entices and allures the affections, be it a long or a short time, do it thus insensibly and imperceptibly, or do the soul take notice of it, we "enter into temptation."

So, then, unto our entering into temptation is required,—

(1.) That by some advantage, or on some occasion, Satan be more earnest than ordinary in his solicitations to sin, by affrightments or allurements, by persecutions or seductions, by himself or others; or that some lust or corruption, by his instigation and advantages of outward objects, provoking, as in prosperity, or terrifying, as in trouble, do tumultuate more than ordinary within us. There is a special acting of the author and principles of temptation required thereunto.

(2.) That the heart be so far entangled with it as to be put to dispute and argue in its own defence, and yet not be wholly able to eject or cast out the poison and leaven that hath been injected; but is surprised, if it be never so little off its watch, into an entanglement not easy to be avoided: so that the soul may cry, and pray, and cry again, and yet not be delivered; as Paul "besought the Lord" thrice for the departure of his temptation, and prevailed not. The entanglement continues. And this usually falls out in one of these two seasons:—

1. When Satan, by the permission of God, for ends best known to himself, hath got some peculiar advantage against the soul; as in the case of Peter,—he sought to winnow him, and prevailed.

2. When a man's lusts and corruptions meet with peculiarly provoking objects and occasions, through the condition of life that a man is in, with the circumstances of it; as it was with David: of both which afterward.

In this state of things, a man is entered into temptation; and this is called the "hour of temptation," Rev. iii. 10,—the season wherein it grows to a head: the discovery whereof will give farther light into the present inquiry, about what it is to "enter into temptation;" for when the hour of temptation is come upon us, we are entered into it. Every great and pressing temptation hath its hour, a season wherein it grows to a head, wherein it is most vigorous, active, operative, and prevalent. It may be long in rising, it may be long urging, more or less; but it hath a season wherein, from the conjunction of other occurences, such as those mentioned, outward or inward, it hath a dangerous hour; and then, for the most part, men enter into it. Hence that very temptation, which at one time hath little or no power on a man,—he can despise it, scorn the motions of it, easily resist it,—at another, bears him away quite before it. It hath, from other circumstances and occurrences, got new strength and efficacy, or the man is enervated and weakened; the hour is come, he is entered into it, and it prevails. David probably had temptations before, in his younger days, to adultery or murder, as he had in the case of Nabal; but the hour of temptation was not come, it had not got its advantages about it, and so he escaped until afterward. Let men look for it that are exposed unto temptations, as who is not? They will have a season wherein their solicitations will be more urgent, their reasonings more plausible, pretences more glorious, hopes of recovery more appearing, opportunities more broad and open, the doors of evil made more beautiful than ever they have been. Blessed is he who is prepared for such a season; without which there is no escaping. This, as I said, is the first thing required to entering into temptation; if we stay here, we are safe.

Before I descend to other particulars, having now entered hereon, I shall show in general,—1st. How or by what means commonly any temptation attains its hour; 2dly. How we may know when any temptation is come to its high noon, and is in its hour.

1st. It doth the first by several ways:—

(1st.) By long solicitations, causing the mind frequently to converse with the evil solicited unto, it begets extenuating thoughts of it. If it makes this process, it is coming towards it hour. It may be when first it began to press upon the soul, the soul was amazed with the ugly appearance of what it aimed at, and cried, "Am I a dog?" If this indignation be not daily heightened, but the soul, by conversing with the evil, begins to grow, as it were, familiar with it, not to be startled as formerly, but rather inclines to cry, "Is it not a little one?" then the temptation is coming towards it high noon; lust hath then enticed and entangled, and is ready to "conceive," James i. 15: of which more at large afterward, in our inquiry how we may know whether we are entered into temptation or no. Our present inquest is after the hour and power of temptation itself.

(2dly.) When it hath prevailed on others, and the soul is not filled with dislike and abhorrency of them and their ways, nor with pity and prayer for their deliverance. This proves an advantage unto it, and raises it towards its height. When that temptation sets upon any one which, at the same time, hath possessed and prevailed with many, it hath so great and so many advantages thereby, that it is surely growing towards its hour. Its prevailing with others is a means to give it its hour against us. The falling off of Hymeneus and Philetus is said to "overthrow the faith of some," 2 Tim. ii. 17-18.

(3dly.) By complicating itself with many considerations that, perhaps, are not absolutely evil. So did the temptation of the Galatians to fall from the purity of the gospel,—freedom from persecution, union and consent with the Jews. Things in themselves good were pleaded in it, and gave life to the temptation itself. But I shall not now insist on the several advantages that any temptation hath to heighten and greaten itself, to make itself prevalent and effectual with the contribution that it receives to this purpose from various circumstances, opportunities, specious pleas and pretences, necessities for the doing that which cannot be done without answering the temptation, and the like; because I must speak unto some of them afterward.

2dly. For the second, it may be known,—

(1st.) By its restless urgency and arguing. When a temptation is in its hour it is restless; it is the time of battle, and it gives the soul no rest. Satan sees his advantage, considers his conjunction of forces, and knows that he must now prevail, or be hopeless for ever. Here are opportunities, here are advantages, here are specious pleas and pretences; some ground is already got by former arguings; here are extenuations of the evil, hopes of pardon by after endeavours, all in a readiness: if he can do nothing now, he must sit down lost in his undertakings. So when he had got all things in a readiness against Christ, he made it the "hour of darkness." When a temptation discovers "mille nocendi artes," presses within doors by imaginations and reasonings, without by solicitations, advantages, and opportunities, let the soul know that the hour of it is come, and the glory of God, with its own welfare, depends on its behaviour in this trial; as we shall see in the particular cases following.

(2dly.) When it makes a conjunction of affrightments and allurements, these two comprise the whole forces of temptation. When both are brought together, temptation is in its hour. They were both in David's case as to the murder of Uriah. There was the fear of his revenge on his wife, and possibly on himself, and fear of the publication of his sin at least; and there was the allurement of his present enjoyment of her whom he lusted after. Men sometimes are carried into sin by love to it, and are continued in it by fear of what will ensue upon it. But in any case, where these two meet, something allures us, something affrights us, and the reasonings that run between them are ready to entangle us,—then is the hour of temptation.

This, then, it is to "enter into temptation," this is the "hour" of it; of which more in the process of our discourse.

III. There is means of prevention prescribed by our Saviour; they are two:—1. "Watch;" 2. "Pray."

1. The first is a general expression by no means to be limited to its native signification of waking from sleep; to watch is as much as to be on our guard, to take heed, to consider all ways and means as to be on our guard, to take heed, to consider all ways and means whereby an enemy may approach to us: so the apostle, 1 Cor. xvi. 13. This it is to "watch" in this business, to "stand fast in the faith," as good soldiers, to "quit ourselves like men." It is as much as prosechein, to "take heed," or look to ourselves, as the same thing is by our Saviour often expressed; so Rev. iii. 2. A universal carefulness and diligence, exercising itself in and by all ways and means prescribed by God, over our hearts and ways, the baits and methods of Satan, the occasions and advantages of sin in the world, that we be not entangled, is that which in this word is presseth on us.

2. For the second direction, of prayer, I need not speak to it. The duty and its concernments are known to all. I shall only add, that these two comprise the whole endeavour of faith for the soul's preservation from temptation.

Chapter 3

Having thus opened the words in the foregoing chapters so far as is necessary to discover the foundation of the truth to be insisted on and improved, I shall lay it down in the ensuing observation:—

It is the great duty of all believers to use all diligence in the ways of Christ's appointment, that they fall not into temptation.

I know God is "able to deliver the godly out of temptations;" I know he is "faithful not to suffer us to be tempted above what we are able, but will make a way for our escape:" yet I dare say I shall convince all those who will attend unto what is delivered and written, that it is our great duty and concernment to use all diligence, watchfulness, and care, that we enter not into temptation; and I shall evince it by the ensuing considerations:—

1. In that compendious instruction given us by our Saviour concerning what we ought to pray for, this of not entering into temptation is expressly one head. Our Saviour knew of what concernment it was to us not to "enter into temptation," when he gave us this as one special subject of our daily dealing with God, Matt. vi. 13. And the order of the words shows us of what importance it is: "Lead us not into temptation, but deliver us from evil." If we are led into temptation, evil will befall us, more or less. How God may be said to tempt us, or to "lead us into temptation," I showed before. In this direction, it is not so much the not giving us up to it, as the powerful keeping us from it that is intended. The last words are, as it were, exegetical, or expository of the former: "Lead us not into temptation, but deliver us from evil;"—"So deal with us that we may be powerfully delivered from that evil which attends our entering into temptation." Our blessed Saviour knows full well our state and condition; he knows the power of temptations, having had experience

of it, Heb. ii. 18; he knows our vain confidence, and the reserves we have concerning our ability to deal with temptations, as he found it in Peter; but he knows our weakness and folly, and how soon we are cast to the ground, and therefore doth he lay in this provision for instruction at the entrance of his ministry, to make us heedful, if possible, in that which is of so great concernment to us. If, then, we will repose any confidence in the wisdom, love, and care of Jesus Christ towards us, we must grant the truth pleaded for.

2. Christ promiseth this freedom and deliverance as a great reward of most acceptable obedience, Rev. iii. 10. This is the great promise made to the church of Philadelphia, wherein Christ found nothing that he would blame, "Thou shalt be kept from the hour of temptation." Not, "Thou shalt be preserved in it;" but he goes higher, "Thou shalt be kept from it." "There is," saith our Saviour, "an hour of temptation coming; a season that will make havoc in the world: multitudes shall then fall from the faith, deny and blaspheme me. Oh, how few will be able to stand and hold out! Some will be utterly destroyed, and perish for ever. Some will get wounds to their souls that shall never be well healed whilst they live in this world, and have their bones broken, so as to go halting all their days. But," saith he, "?because thou hast kept the word of my patience,' I will be tender towards thee, and keep thee from this hour of temptation.'?" Certainly that which Christ thus promises to his beloved church, as a reward of her service, love, and obedience, is no light thing. Whatever Christ promiseth to his spouse is a fruit of unspeakable love; that is so in an especial manner which is promised as a reward of special obedience.

3. Let us to this purpose consider the general issues of men's entering into temptation, and that of bad and good men, of ungrounded professors, and of the choicest saints.

(1.) For the first I shall offer but one or two texts of Scripture. Luke viii. 13, "They on the rock are they, which, when they hear, receive the word with joy, and have no root, but for a while believe."

Well! how long do they believe? They are affected with the preaching of the word, and believe thereon, make profession, bring forth some fruits; but until when do they abide? Says he, "In the time of temptation they fall away." When once they enter into temptation they are gone for ever. Temptation withers all their profession, and slays their souls. We see this accomplished every day. Men who have attended on the preaching of the gospel, been affected and delighted with it, that have made profession of it, and have been looked on, it may be, as believers, and thus have continued for some years; no sooner doth temptation befall them that hath vigour and permanency in it, but they are turned out of the way, and are gone for ever. They fall to hate the word they have delighted in, despise the professors of it, and are hardened by sin. So Matt. vii. 26, "He that heareth these sayings of mine, and doeth that not, is like unto a foolish man, which built his house upon the sand." But what doth this house of profession do? It shelters him, keeps him warm, and stands for a while. But saith he, verse 27, "When the rain descends, when temptation comes, it falls utterly, and its fall is great." Judas follows our Saviour three years, and all goes well with him: he no sooner enters into temptation, Satan hath got him and winnowed him, but he is gone. Demas will preach the gospel until the love of the world befall him, and he is utterly turned aside. It were endless to give instances of this. Entrance into temptation is, with this sort of men, an entrance into apostasy, more or less, in part or in whole; it faileth not.

(2.) For the saints of God themselves, let us see, by some instances, what issue they have had of their entering into temptation. I shall name a few:—

Adam was the "son of God," Luke iii. 38, created in the image of God, full of that integrity, righteousness, and holiness, which might be and was an eminent resemblance of the holiness of God. He had a far greater inherent stock of ability than we, and had nothing in him to entice or seduce him; yet this Adam no sooner enters into temptation but he is gone, lost, and ruined, he and all his posterity with him. What can we expect in the like condition, that have not only in our temptations, as he had, a cunning devil to deal withal, but a cursed world and a corrupt heart also?

Abraham was the father of the faithful, whose faith is proposed as a pattern to all them that shall believe; yet he, entering twice into the same temptation, namely, that of fear about his wife, was twice overpowered by it, to the dishonour of God, and no doubt the disquietment of his own soul, Gen. xii. 12, 13, xx. 2.

David is called a "man after God's own heart" by God himself; yet what a dreadful thing is the story of his entering into temptation! He is no sooner entangled, but he is plunged into adultery; thence seeking deliverance by his own invention, like a poor creature in a toil, he is entangled more and more, until he lies as one dead, under the power of sin and folly.

I might mention Noah, Lot, Hezekiah, Peter, and the rest, whose temptations and falls therein are on record for our instruction. Certainly he that hath any heart in these things cannot but say, as the inhabitants of Samaria upon the letter of Jehu, "?Behold, two kings stood not before him, how shall we stand?' O Lord, if such mighty pillars have been cast to the ground, such cedars blown down, how shall I stand before temptations? Oh, keep me that I enter not in!" "Vestigia terrent." Behold the footsteps of them that have gone in. Whom do you see retiring without a wound? a blemish at least? On this account would the apostle have us to exercise tenderness towards them that are fallen into sin: Gal. vi. 1, "Considering thyself, lest thou also be tempted." He doth not say, "Lest thou also sin, or fall, or seest the power of temptation in others, and knowest not how soon thou mayst be tempted, nor what will be the state and condition of thy soul thereupon." Assuredly, he that hath seen so many better, stronger men than himself fail, and cast down in the trial, will think it incumbent on him to remember the battle, and, if it be possible, to come there no more. Is it not a madness for a man that can scarce crawl up and down, he is so weak (which is the case of most of us), if he avoid not what he hath seen giants foiled in the undertaking of? Thou art yet whole and sound; take heed of temptation, lest it be with thee as it was with Abraham, David, Lot, Peter, Hezekiah, the Galatians, who fell in the time of trial.

In nothing doth the folly of the hearts of men show itself more openly, in the days wherein we live, than in this cursed boldness, after so many warnings from God, and so many sad experiences every day under their eyes, of running into and putting themselves upon temptations. Any society, any company, any conditions of outward advantages, without once weighing what their strength, or what the concernment of their poor souls is, they are ready for. Though they go over the dead and the slain that in those ways and paths but even now fell down before them, yet they will go on without regard or trembling. At this door are gone out hundreds, thousands of professors, within a few years. But,—

4. Let us consider ourselves,—what our weakness is; and what temptation is,—its power and efficacy, with what it leads unto:—

(1.) For ourselves, we are weakness itself. We have no strength, no power to withstand. Confidence of any strength in us is one great part of our weakness; it was so in Peter. He that says he can do any thing, can do nothing as he should. And, which is worse, it is the worst kind of weakness that is in us,—a weakness from treachery,—a weakness arising from that party which every temptation hath in us. If a castle or fort be never so strong and well fortified, yet if there be a treacherous party within, that is ready to betray it on every opportunity, there is no preserving it from the enemy. There are traitors in our hearts, ready to take part, to close, and side with every temptation, and to give up all to them; yea, to solicit and bribe temptations to do the work, as traitors incite an enemy. Do not flatter yourselves that you should hold out; there are secret lusts that lie lurking in your hearts, which perhaps now stir not, which, as soon as any temptation befalls you, will rise, tumultuate, cry, disquiet, seduce, and never give over until they are either killed or satisfied. He that promises himself that the frame of his heart will be the same under a temptation as it is before will be wofully mistaken. "Am I a dog, that I should do this thing?" says Hazael. Yea, thou wilt be such a dog if ever thou be king of Syria; temptation from thy interest will unman thee. He that now abhors the thoughts of such and such a thing, if he once enters into temptation will find his heart inflamed towards it, and all contrary reasonings overborne and silenced. He will deride his former fears, cast out his scruples, and contemn the consideration that he lived upon. Little did Peter think he should deny and forswear his Master so soon as ever he was questioned whether he knew him or no. It was no better when the hour of temptation came; all resolutions were forgotten, all love to Christ buried; the present temptation closing with his carnal fear carried all before it.

To handle this a little more distinctly, I shall consider the means of safety from the power of temptation, if we enter therein, that may be expected from ourselves; and that in general as to the spring and rise of them, and in particular as to the ways of exerting that strength we have, or seem to have:—

1. In general, all we can look for is from our hearts. What a man's heart is, that is he; but now what is the heart of a man in such a season?

1st. Suppose a man is not a believer, but only a professor of the gospel, what can the heart of such a one do? Prov. x. 20, "The heart of the wicked is little worth;" and surely that which is little worth in any thing is not much worth in this. A wicked man may in outward things be of great use; but come to his heart, that is false and a thing of nought. Now, withstanding of temptation is heartwork; and when it comes like a flood, can such a rotten trifle as a wicked man's heart stand before it? But of these before. Entering into temptation and apostasy is the same with them.

2dly. Let it be whose heart it will, Prov. xxviii. 26, "He that trusteth in his own heart is a fool;" he that doth so, be he what he will, in that he is foolish. Peter did so in his temptation; he trusted in his own heart: "Though all men forsake thee, I will not." It was his folly; but why was it his folly? He shall not be delivered; it will not preserve him in snares; it will not deliver him in temptations. The heart of a man will promise him very fair before a temptation comes. "Am I a dog," says Hazael, "that I should do this thing?" "Though all men should deny thee," [says Peter,] "I will not. Shall I do this evil? It cannot be." All the arguments that are suited to give check to the heart in such a condition are mustered up. Did not Peter, think you, do so? "What! deny my Master, the Son of God, my Redeemer, who loves me? Can such ingratitude, unbelief, rebellion, befall me? I will not do it." Shall, then, a man rest in it that his heart will be steadfast? Let the wise man answer: "He that trusteth in his own heart is a fool." "The heart is deceitful," Jer. xvii. 9. We would not willingly trust any thing wherein there is any deceit or guile; here is that which is "deceitful above all things." It hath a thousand shifts and treacheries that is will deal withal; when it comes to the trial, every temptation will steal it away, Hos. iv. 11. Generally men's hearts deceive them no oftener than they do trust in them, and then they never fail so to do.

2. Consider the particular ways and means that such a heart hath or can use to safeguard itself in the hour of temptation, and their insufficiency to that purpose will quickly appear. I shall instance in some few only:—

1st. Love of honour in the world. Reputation and esteem in the church, obtained by former profession and walking, is one of the heart's own weapons to defend itself in the hour of temptation. "Shall such a one as I fly? I who have had such a reputation in the church of God, shall I now lose it by giving way to this lust, to this temptation? by closing with this or that public evil?" This consideration hath such an influence on the spirits of some, that they think it will be a shield and buckler against any assaults that may befall them. They will die a thousand times before they will forfeit that repute they have in the church of God! But, alas! this is but a withe, or a new cord, to bind a giant temptation withal. What think you of the "third part of the stars of heaven?" Rev. xii. 4. Had they not shone in the firmament of the church? Were they not sensible, more than enough, of their own honour, height, usefulness, and reputation? But when the dragon comes with his temptations, he casts them down to the earth. Yea, great temptations will make men, who have not a better defence, insensibly fortify themselves against that dishonour and disreputation that their ways are attended withal. "Populus sibilet, at mihi plaudo." Do we not know instances yet living of some who have ventured on compliance with wicked men after the glory of a long and useful profession, and within a while, finding themselves cast down thereby from their reputation with the saints, have hardened themselves against it and ended in apostasy? as John xv. 6. This kept not Judas; it kept not Hymeneus nor Philetus; it kept not the stars of heaven; nor will it keep thee.

2dly. There is, on the other side, the consideration of shame, reproach, loss, and the like. This also men may put their trust in as a defence against temptations, and do not fear but to be safeguarded and preserved by it. They would not for the world bring that shame and reproach upon themselves that such and such miscarriages are attended withal! Now, besides that this consideration extends itself only to open sins, such as the world takes notice of and abhors, and so is of no use at all in such cases as wherein pretences and colours may be invented and used, nor in public temptations to loose and careless walking, like those of our days, nor in cases that may be disputable in themselves, though expressly sinful to the consciences of persons under temptations, nor in heart sins,—in all which and most other cases of temptation there are innumerable reliefs ready to be tendered unto the heart against this consideration; besides all this, I say, we see by experience how easily this cord is broken when once the heart begins to be entangled. Each corner of the land if full of examples to this purpose.

3dly. They have yet that which outweighs these lesser considerations,—namely, that they will not wound their own consciences, and disturb their peace, and bring themselves in danger of hell fire. This, surely, if any thing, will preserve men in the hour of temptation. They will not lavish away their peace, nor venture their souls by running on God and the thick bosses of his buckler! What can be of more efficacy and prevalency? I confess this is of great importance; and oh that it were more pondered than it is! that we laid more weight upon the preservation of our peace with God than we do! yet I say that even this consideration in him who is otherwhere off from his watch, and doth not make it his work to follow the other rules insisted on, it will not preserve him; for,—

(1st.) The peace of such a one may be false peace or security, made up of presumption and false hopes; yea, though he be a believer, it may be so. Such was David's peace after his sin, before Nathan came to him; such was Laodicea's peace when ready to perish; and Sardis her peace when dying. What should secure a soul that it is otherwise, seeing, it is supposed, that it doth not universally labour to keep the word of Christ's patience, and to be watchful in all things? Think you that the peace of many in these days will be found to be true peace at last? Nothing less. They go alive down to hell, and death will have dominion over them in the morning. Now, if a man's peace be such, do you think that can preserve him which cannot preserve itself? It will give way at the first vigorous assault of a temptation in its height and hour. Like a broken reed, it will run into the hand of him that leaneth on it. But,—

(2dly.) Suppose the peace cared for, and proposed to safeguard the soul, be true and good, yet when all is laid up in this one bottom, when the hour of temptation comes, so many reliefs will be tendered against this consideration as will make it useless. "This evil is small; it is questionable; it falls not openly and downright upon conscience. I do but fear consequences; it may be I may be keep my peace notwithstanding. Others of the people of God have fallen, and yet kept or recovered their peace. If it be lost for a season, it may be obtained again. I will not solicit its station any more; or though peace be lost, safety may remain." And a thousand such pleas there are, which are all planted as batteries against this fort, so that it cannot long hold out.

(3dly.) The fixing on this particular only is to make good one passage or entrance, whilst the enemy assaults us round about. It is true, a little armour would serve to defend a man if he might choose there his enemy should strike him; but we are commanded to take the "whole armour of God" if we intend to resist and stand, Eph. vi. This we speak of is but one piece; and when our eye is only to that, temptation may enter and prevail twenty other ways. For instance, a man may be tempted to worldliness, unjust gain, revenge, vain-glory, or the like. If he fortify himself alone with this consideration, he will not do this thing, and wound his conscience and lose his peace; fixing his eye on this particular, and counting himself safe whilst he is not overcome on that hand, it may be neglect of private communion with God, sensuality, and the like, do creep in, and he is not one jot in a better condition than if he had fallen under the power of that part of the temptation which was most visibly pressing on him. Experience gives to see that this doth and will fail also. There is no saint of God but puts a valuation on the peace he hath; yet how many of them fail in the day of temptation!

(4thly.) But yet they have another consideration also, and that is, the vileness of sinning against God. How shall they do this thing, and sin against God, the God of their mercies, of their salvation? How shall they wound Jesus Christ, who died for them? This surely cannot but preserve them. I answer,—

First, We see every day this consideration failing also. There is no child of God that is overcome of temptation but overcomes this consideration. It is not, then, a sure and infallible defensative.

Secondly, This consideration is twofold: either it expresses the thoughts of the soul with particular reference to the temptation contended withal and then it will not preserve it; or it expresses the universal, habitual frame of heart that is in us, upon all accounts, and then it falleth in with what I shall tender as the universal medicine and remedy in this case in the process of this discourse; whereof afterward.

(2.) Consider the power of temptation, partly from what was showed before, from the effects and fruits of it in the saints of old, partly from such other effects in general as we find ascribed to it; as,—

1. It will darken the mind, that a man shall not be able to make a right judgement of things, so as he did before he entered into it. As in the men of the world, the god of this world blinds their minds that they should not see the glory of Christ in the gospel, 2 Cor. iv. 4, and "whoredom, and wine, and new wine, take away their hearts," Hos. iv. 11; so it is in the nature of every temptation, more or less, to take away the heart, or to darken the understanding of the person tempted.

And this it doth divers ways:—

1st. By fixing the imagination and the thoughts upon the object whereunto it tends, so that the mind shall be diverted from the consideration of the things that would relieve and succour it in the state wherein it is. A man is tempted to apprehend that he is forsaken of God, that he is an object of his hatred, that he hath no interest in Christ. By the craft of Satan the mind shall be so fixed to the consideration of this state and condition, with the distress of it, that he shall not be able to manage any of the reliefs suggested and tendered to him against it; but, following the fulness of his own thoughts, shall walk on in darkness and have no light. I say, a temptation will so possess and fill the mind with thoughtfulness of itself and the matter of it, that it will take off from that clear consideration of things which otherwise it might and would have. And those things whereof the mind was wont to have a vigorous sense, to keep it from sin, will by this means come to have no force or efficacy with it; nay, it will commonly bring men to that state and condition, that when others, to whom their estate is known, are speaking to them the things that concern their deliverance and peace, their minds will be so possessed with the matter of their temptation as not at all to understand, scarce to hear one word, that is spoken to them.

2dly. By woful entangling of the affections; which, when they are engaged, what influence they have in blinding the mind and darkness and darkening the understanding is known. If any know it not, let him but open his eyes in these days, and he will quickly learn it. By what ways and means it is that engaged affections will becloud the mind and darken it I shall not now declare; only, I say, give me a man engaged in hope, love, fear, in reference to any particulars wherein he ought not, and I shall quickly show you wherein he is darkened and blinded. This, then, you will fail in if you enter into temptation:—The present judgment you have of things will not be utterly altered, but darkened and rendered infirm to influence the will and master the affections. These, being set at liberty by temptation, will run on in madness. Forthwith detestation of sin, abhorring of it, terror of the Lord, sense of love, presence of Christ crucified, all depart, and leave the heart a prey to its enemy.

3dly. Temptation will give oil and fuel to our lusts,—incite, provoke, and make then tumultuate and rage beyond measure. Tendering a lust, a corruption, a suitable object, advantage, occasion, it heightens and exasperates it, makes it for a season wholly predominant: so dealt it with carnal fear in Peter, with pride in Hezekiah, with covetousness in Achan, with uncleanness in David, with worldliness in Demas, with ambition in Diotrephes. It will lay the reins on the neck of a lust, and put to the sides of it, that it may rush forward like a horse into the battle. A man knows not the pride, fury, madness of a corruption, until it meet with a suitable temptation. And what now will a poor soul think to do? His mind is darkened, his affections entangled, his lusts inflamed and provoked, his relief is defeated; and what will be the issue of such a condition?

(3.) Consider that temptations are either public or private; and let us a little view the efficacy and power of them apart:—

1. There are public temptations; such as that mentioned, Rev. iii. 10, that was to come upon the world, "to try them that dwell upon the earth;" or a combination of persecution and seduction for the trial of a careless generation of professors. Now, concerning such a temptation, consider that,—
2.

1st. It hath an efficacy in respect of God, who sends it to revenge the neglect and contempt of the gospel on the one hand, and treachery of false professors on the other. Hence it will certainly accomplish what it receives commission from him to do. When Satan offered his service to go forth and seduce Ahab that he might fall, God says to him, "Thou shalt persuade him, and prevail also: go forth, and do so," 1 Kings xxii. 22. He is permitted as to his wickedness, and commissionated as to the event and punishment intended. When the Christian world was to be given up to folly and false worship for their neglect of the truth, and their naked, barren, fruitless, Christ-dishonouring profession, it is said of the temptation that fell upon then, that "God sent them strong delusion, that they should believe a lie," 2 Thess. ii. 11. That that comes so from God in a judiciary manner, hath a power with it and shall prevail. That selfish spiritually-slothful, careless , and worldly frame of spirit, which in these days hath infected almost the body of professors, if it have a commission from God to kill hypocrites, to wound negligent saints, to break their bones, and make them scandalous, that they may be ashamed, shall it not have a power and efficacy so to do? What work hath the spirit of error made amongst us! Is it not from hence, that as some men delighted not to retain God in their hearts, so he hath "given them up to a reprobate mind," Rom. i. 28. A man would think it strange, yea, it is matter of amazement, to see persons of a sober spirit, pretending to great things in the ways of God, overcome, captivated, ensnared, destroyed by weak means, sottish opinions, foolish imaginations, such as a man would think it impossible that they should ever lay hold on sensible or rational men, much less on professors of the gospel. But that which God will have to be strong, let us not think weak. No strength but the strength of God can stand in the way of the weakest things of the world that are commissionated from God for any end or purpose whatever.

2dly. There is in such temptations the secret insinuation of examples in those that are accounted godly and are professors: Matt. xxiv. 12, "Because iniquity shall abound, the love of many shall wax cold," etc. The abounding of iniquity in some will insensibly cast water on the zeal and love of others, that by little and little it shall wax cold. Some begin to grow negligent, careless, worldly, wanton. They break the ice towards the pleasing of the flesh. At first their love also waxes cold; and the brunt being over, they also conform to them, and are cast into the same mould with them. "A little leaven leaveneth the whole lump." Paul repeats this saying twice, 1 Cor. v. 6, and Gal. v. 9. He would have us take notice of it; and it is of the danger of the infection of the whole body, from the ill examples of some, whereof he speaks. We know how insensibly leaven proceedeth to give savour to the whole; so it is termed a "root of bitterness" that "springeth up and defileth many," Heb. xii. 15. If one little piece of leaven, if one bitter root, may endanger the whole, how much more when there are many roots of that nature, and much leaven is scattered abroad! It is easy following a multitude to do evil, and saying "A conspiracy" to them to whom the people say "A conspiracy." Would any one have thought it possible that such and such professors, in our days, should have fallen into ways of self, of flesh, of the world? to play at cards, dice, revel, dance? to neglect family, closet duties? to be proud, haughty, ambitious, worldly, covetous, oppressive? or that they should be turned away after foolish, vain, ridiculous opinions, deserting the gospel of Christ? In which two lies the great temptation that is come on us, the inhabitants of this world, to try us. But doth not every man see that this is come to pass? And may we not see how it is come to pass? Some loose, empty professors, who had never more than a form of godliness, when they had served their turn of that, began the way to them; then others began a little to comply, and to please the flesh in so doing. This, by little and little, hath reached even the top boughs and branches of our profession, until almost all flesh hath corrupted its way. And he that departeth from these iniquities makes his name a prey, if not his person.

3dly. Public temptations are usually accompanied with strong reasons and pretences, that are too hard for men, or at least insensibly prevail upon them to an undervaluation of the evil whereunto the temptation leads, to give strength to that complicated temptation which in these days hath even cast down the people of God from their excellency,—hath cut their locks, and made them become like other men. How full is the world of specious pretences and pleadings! As there is the liberty and freedom of Christians, delivered from a bondage frame, this is a door that, in my own observation, I have seen sundry going out at, into sensuality and apostasy; beginning at a light conversation, proceeding to a neglect of the Sabbath, public and private duties, ending in dissoluteness and profaneness. And then there is leaving of public things to Providence, being contented with what is;—things good in themselves, but disputed into wretched, carnal compliances, and the utter ruin of all zeal for God, the interest of Christ or his people in the world. These and the like considerations, joined with the ease and plenty, the greatness and promotion of professors, have so brought things about, that whereas we have by Providence shifted places with the men of the world, we have by sin shifted spirits with them also. We are like a plantation of men carried into a foreign country. In a short space they degenerate from the manners of the people from whence they came, and fall into that thing in the soil and the air that transformed them. Give me leave a little to follow my similitude: He that should see the prevailing party of these nations, many of those in rule, power, favour, with all their adherents, and remember that they were a colony of Puritans,—whose habitation was "in a low place," as the prophet speaks of the city of God,—translated by a high hand to the mountains they now possess, cannot but wonder how soon they have forgot the customs, manners, ways, of their own old people, and are cast into the mould of them that went before them in the places whereunto they are translated. I speak of us all, especially of us who are amongst the lowest of the people, where perhaps this iniquity doth most abound. What were those before us that we are not? what did they that we do not? Prosperity hath slain the foolish and wounded the wise.

2. Suppose the temptation is private. This hath been spoken to before; I shall add two things:—

1st. Its union and incorporation with lust, whereby it gets within the soul, and lies at the bottom of its actings. John tells us, 1 Epist. ii. 16, that the things that are "in the world" are, "the lust of the flesh, the lust of the eyes, the pride of life." Now, it is evident that all these things are principally in the subject, not in the object,—in the heart, not in the world. But they are said to be "in the world," because the world gets into them, mixes itself with them, unites, incorporates. As faith and the promises are said to be "mixed," Heb. iv. 2, so are lust and temptation mixed: they twine together; receive mutual improvement from one another; grow each of them higher and higher by the mutual strength they administer to one another. Now, by this means temptation gets so deep in the heart that no contrary reasonings can reach unto it; nothing but what can kill the lust can conquer the temptation. Like leprosy that hath mingled itself with the wall, the wall itself must be pulled down, or the leprosy will not be cured. Like a gangrene that mixes poison with the blood and spirits, and cannot be separated from the place where it is, but both must be cut off together. For instance, in David's temptation to uncleanness, ten thousand considerations might have been taken in to stop the mouth of the temptation; but it had united itself with his lust, and nothing but the killing of that could destroy it, or get him the conquest. This deceives many a one. They have some pressing temptation, that, having got some advantages, is urgent upon them. They pray against it, oppose it with all powerful considerations, such as whereof every one seems sufficient to conquer and destroy it, at least to overpower it, that it should never be troublesome any more; but no good is done, no ground is got or obtained, yea, it grows upon them more and more. What is the reason of it? It hath incorporated and united itself with the lust, and is safe from all the opposition they make. If they would make work indeed, they are to set upon the whole of the lust itself; their ambition, pride, worldliness, sensuality, or whatever it be, that the temptation is united with. All other dealings with it are like tamperings with a prevailing gangrene: the part or whole may be preserved a little while, in great torment; excision or death must come at last. The soul may cruciate itself for a season with such a procedure; but it must come to this,—its lust must die, or the soul must die.

2dly. In what part soever of the soul the lust be seated wherewith the temptation is united, it draws after it the whole soul by one means or other, and so prevents or anticipates any opposition. Suppose it be a lust of the mind,—as there are lusts of the mind and uncleanness of the spirit, such as ambition, vain-glory, and the like,—what a world of ways hath the understanding to bridle the affections that they should not so tenaciously cleave to God, seeing in what it aimeth at there is so much to give them contentment and satisfaction! It will not only prevent all the reasonings of the mind, which it doth necessarily,—being like a bloody infirmity in the eyes, presenting all things to the common sense and perception in that hue and colour,—but it will draw the whole soul, on other accounts and collateral considerations, into the same frame. It promises the whole a share in the spoil aimed at; as Judas's money, that he first desired from covetousness, was to be shared among all his lusts. Or be it in the more sensual part, and first possesseth the affections,—what prejudices they will bring upon the understanding, how they will bribe it to an acquiescence, what arguments, what hopes they will supply it withal, cannot easily be expressed, as was before showed. In brief, there is no particular temptation, but, when it is in its hour, it hath such a contribution of assistance from things good, evil, indifferent, is fed by so many considerations that seem to be most alien and foreign to it, in some cases hath such specious pleas and pretences, that its strength will easily be acknowledged.

(4.) Consider the end of any temptation; this is Satan's end and sin's end,—that is, the dishonour of God and the ruin of our souls.

(5.) Consider what hath been the issue of thy former temptations that thou hast had. Have they not defiled thy conscience, disquieted thy peace, weakened thee in thy obedience, clouded the face of God? Though thou wast not prevailed on to the outward evil or utmost issue of thy temptation, yet hast thou not been foiled? hath not thy soul been sullied and grievously perplexed with it? yea, didst thou ever in thy life come fairly off, without sensible loss, from any temptation almost that thou hadst to deal withal; and wouldst thou willingly be entangled again? If thou art at liberty, take heed; enter no more, if it be possible, lest a worse thing happen to thee.

These, I say, are some of those many considerations that might be insisted on, to manifest the importance of the truth proposed, and the fulness of our concernment in taking care that we "enter not into temptation."

Against what hath been spoken, some objections that secretly insinuate themselves into the souls of men, and have an efficacy to make them negligent and careless in this thing, which is of such importance to them,—a duty of such indispensable necessity to them who intend to walk with God in any peace, or with any faithfulness,—are to be considered and removed. And they are these that follow:—

Obj. 1. "Why should we so fear and labour to avoid temptation? James i. 2, we are commanded to count it all joy when we fall into divers temptations.' Now, certainly I need not solicitously avoid the falling into that which, when I am fallen into, I am to count it all joy." To which I answer,—

1. You will not hold by this rule in all things,—namely, that a man need not seek to avoid that which, when he cannot but fall into, it is his duty to rejoice therein. The same apostle bids the rich "rejoice that they are made low," chap. i. 10. And, without doubt, to him who is acquainted with the goodness, and wisdom, and love of God in his dispensations, in every condition that is needful for him, it will be a matter of rejoicing to him: but yet, how few rich, godly men can you persuade not to take heed, and use all lawful means that they be not made poor and low! and, in most cases, the truth is, it were their sin not to do so. It is our business to make good our stations, and to secure ourselves as we can; if God alter our condition we are to rejoice in it. If the temptations here mentioned befall us, we may have cause to rejoice; but not if, by a neglect of duty, we fall into them.

2. Temptations are taken two ways:—

(1.) Passively and merely materially, for such things as are, or in some cases may be, temptations; or,—

(2.) Actively, for such as do entice to sin. James speaks of temptations in the first sense only; for having said, "Count it all joy when ye fall into divers temptations," verse 2; he adds, verse 12, "Blessed is the man that endureth temptation: for when he is tried, he shall receive the crown of life." But now whereas a man might say, "If this be so, then temptations are good, and from God;"—"No," says James; "take temptation in such a sense as that it is a thing enticing and leading to sin, so God tempts none; but every man is tempted of his own lust," verse 13, 14. "To have such temptations, to be tempted to sin, that is not the blessed thing I intend; but the enduring of afflictions that God sends for the trial of our faith, that is a blessed thing. So that, though I must count it all joy when, through the will of God, I fall into divers afflictions for my trial, which yet have the matter of temptation in them, yet I am to use all care and diligence that my lust have no occasions or advantages given unto it to tempt me to sin."

Obj. 2. "But was not our Saviour Christ himself tempted; and is it evil to be brought into the same state and condition with him? Yea, it is not only said that he was tempted, but his being so is expressed as a thing advantageous, and conducing to his mercifulness as our priest: Heb. ii. 17, 18, In that he himself hath suffered, being tempted, he is able to succour them that are tempted.' And he makes it a ground of a great promise to his disciples, that they had abode with him in his temptations,' Luke xxii. 28."

Ans. It is true, our Saviour was tempted; but yet his temptations are reckoned among the evils that befell him in the days of his flesh,—things that came on him through the malice of the world and the prince thereof. He did not wilfully cast himself into temptation, which he said was "to tempt the Lord our God," Matt. iv. 7; as, indeed, willingly to enter into any temptation is highly to tempt God. Now, our condition is so, that, use the greatest diligence and watchfulness that we can, yet we shall be sure to be tempted, and be made like to Christ therein. This hinders not but that it is our duty to the utmost to prevent our falling into them; and that namely on this account:—Christ had only the suffering part of temptation when he entered into it; we have also the sinning part of it. When the prince of this world came to Christ, he had "no part in him;" but when he comes to us, he hath so in us. So that though in one effect of temptations, namely trials and disquietness, we are made like to Christ, and so are to rejoice as far as by any means that is produced; yet by another we are made unlike to him,—which is our being defiled and entangled: and are therefore to seek by all means to avoid them. We never come off like Christ. Who of us "enter into temptation" and are not defiled?

Obj. 3. "But what need this great endeavour and carefulness? Is it not said that God is faithful, who will not suffer us to be tempted above what we are able, but will with the temptation also make a way to escape?' 1 Cor. x. 13; and He knoweth how to deliver the godly out of temptations,' 2 Pet. ii. 9. What need we, then, be solicitous that we enter not into them?"

Ans. I much question what assistance he will have from God in his temptation who willingly enters into it, because he supposes God hath promised to deliver him out of it. The Lord knows that, through the craft of Satan, the subtlety and malice of the world, the deceitfulness of sin, that doth so easily beset us, when we have done our utmost, yet we shall enter into divers temptations. In his love, care, tenderness, and faithfulness, he hath provided such a sufficiency of grace for us, that they shall not utterly prevail to make an everlasting separation between him and our souls. Yet I have three things to say to this objection:—

(1.) He that wilfully or negligently enters into temptation hath no reason in the world to promise himself any assistance from God, or any deliverance from the temptation whereunto he is entered. The promise is made to them whom temptations do befall in their way, whether they will or not; not them that wilfully fall into them,—that run out of their way to meet with them. And therefore the devil (as is usually observed), when he tempted our Saviour, left out that expression of the text of Scripture, which he wrested to his purpose, "All thy ways." The promise of deliverance is to them who are in their ways; whereof this is one principal, to beware of temptation.

(2.) Though there be a sufficiency of grace provided for all the elect, that they shall by no temptation fall utterly from God, yet it would make any gracious heart to tremble, to think what dishonour to God, what scandal to the gospel, what woful darkness and disquietness they may bring upon their own souls, though they perish not. And they who are scared by nothing but fear of hell, on whom other considerations short thereof have no influence, in my apprehension have more reason to fear it than perhaps they are aware of.

(3.) To enter on temptation on this account is to venture on sin (which is the same with "continuing with sin") "that grace may abound," Rom. vi. 1, 2; which the apostle rejects the thoughts of with greatest detestation. Is it not a madness, for a man willingly to suffer the ship wherein he is to split itself on a rock, to the irrecoverable loss of his merchandise, because he supposes he shall in his own person swim safely to shore on a plank? Is it less in him who will hazard the shipwreck of all his comfort, peace, joy, and so much of the glory of God and honour of the gospel as he is entrusted with, merely on supposition that his soul shall yet escape? These things a man would think did not deserve to be mentioned, and yet with such as these do poor souls sometimes delude themselves.

Chapter 4

Particular cases proposed to consideration—The first, its resolution in sundry particulars—Several discoveries of the state of a soul entering into temptation.

These things being premised in general, I proceed to the consideration of three particular cases arising from the truth proposed: the first whereof relates unto the thing itself; the second unto the time or season thereof; and the last unto deportment in reference unto the prevention of the evil treated of.

First, then, it may be inquired,—

1. How a man may know when he is entered into temptation.

2. What directions are to be given for the preventing of our entering into temptation.

3. What seasons there are wherein a man may and ought to fear that an hour of temptation is at hand.

1. How shall a man know whether he be entered into temptation or no, is our first inquiry. I say, then,—

(1.) When a man is drawn into any sin, he may be sure that he hath entered into temptation. All sin is from temptation, James i. 14. Sin is a fruit that comes only from that root. Though a man be never so suddenly or violently surprised in or with any sin, yet it is from some temptation or other that he hath been so surprised: so the apostle, Gal. vi. 1. If a man be surprised, overtaken with a fault, yet he was tempted to it; for says he, "Consider thyself, lest thou also be tempted,"—that is, as he was when he was so surprised, as it were, at unawares. This men sometimes take no notice of, to their great disadvantage. When they are overtaken with a sin they set themselves to repent of that sin, but do not consider the temptation that was the cause of it, to set themselves against that also to take care that they enter no more into it. Hence are they quickly again entangled by it, though they have the greatest detestation of the sin itself that can be expressed. He that would indeed get the conquest over any sin must consider his temptations to it, and strike at that root; without deliverance from thence, he will not be healed.

This is a folly that possesses many who have yet a quick and living sense of sin. They are sensible of their sins, not of their temptations,—are displeased with the bitter fruit, but cherish the poisonous root. Hence, in the midst of their humiliations for sin, they will continue in those ways, those societies, in the pursuit of those ends, which have occasioned that sin; of which more afterward.

(2.) Temptations have several degrees. Some arise to such an height, do so press on the soul, so cruciate and disquiet it, so fight against all opposition that is made to it, that it is a peculiar power of temptation that he is to wrestle withal. When a fever rages, a man knows he is sick, unless his distemper have made him mad. The lusts of men, as James tells us, "entice, draw away," and seduce them to sin; but this they do of themselves, without peculiar instigation, in a more quiet, even, and sedate manner. If they grow violent, if they hurry the soul up and down, give it no rest, the soul may know that they have got the help of temptation to their assistance.

Take an empty vessel and put it into some stream that is in its course to the sea, it will infallibly be carried thither, according to the course and speed of the stream; but let strong winds arise upon it, it will be driven with violence on every bank and rock, until, being broken in pieces, it is swallowed up of the ocean. Men's lusts will infallibly (if not mortified in the death of Christ) carry them into eternal ruin, but oftentimes without much noise, according to the course of the stream of their corruptions; but let the wind of strong temptations befall them, they are hurried into innumerable scandalous sins, and so, broken upon all accounts, are swallowed up in eternity. So is it in general with men; so in particular. Hezekiah had the root of pride in him always; yet it did not make him run up and down to show his treasure and his riches until he fell into temptation by the ambassadors of the king of Babylon. So had David; yet could he keep off from numbering the people until Satan stood up and provoked him, and solicited him to do it. Judas was covetous from the beginning; yet he did not contrive to satisfy it by selling of his Master until the devil entered into him, and he thereby into temptation. The like may be said of Abraham, Jonah, Peter, and the rest. So that when any lust or corruption whatever tumultuates and disquieteth the soul, puts it with violence on sin, let the soul know that it hath got the advantage of some outward temptation, though as yet it perceiveth not wherein, or at least is become itself a peculiar temptation by some incitation or provocation that hath befallen it, and is to be looked to more than ordinarily.

(3.) Entering into temptation may be seen in the lesser degrees of it; as, for instance, when the heart begins secretly to like the matter of the temptation, and is content to feed it and increase it by any ways that it may without downright sin.

In particular, a man begins to be in repute for piety, wisdom, learning, or the like,—he is spoken of much to that purpose; his heart is tickled to hear of it, and his pride and ambition affected with it. If this man now, with all his strength, ply the things from whence his repute, and esteem, and glory amongst men do spring, with a secret eye to have it increased, he is entering into temptation; which, if he take not heed, will quickly render him a slave of lust. So was it with Jehu. He perceived that his repute for zeal began to grow abroad, and he got honour by it. Jonadab comes in his way, a good and holy man. "Now," thinks Jehu, "I have an opportunity to grow in honour of my zeal." So he calls Jonadab to him, and to work he goes most seriously. The things he did were good in themselves, but he was entered into temptation, and served his lust in that he did. So is it with many scholars. They find themselves esteemed and favoured for their learning. This takes hold of the pride and ambition of their hearts. Hence they set themselves to study with all diligence day and night,—a thing good in itself; but they do it that they might satisfy the thoughts and words of men, wherein they delight: and so in all they do they make provision for the flesh to fulfil the lusts thereof.

It is true, God oftentimes brings light out of this darkness, and turns things to a better issue. After, it may be, a man hath studied sundry years, with an eye upon his lusts,—his ambition, pride, and vain-glory,—rising early and going to bed late, to give them satisfaction, God comes in with his grace, turns the soul to himself, robs those Egyptian lusts, and so consecrates that to the use of the tabernacle which was provided for idols.

Men may be thus entangled in better things than learning, even in the profession of piety, in their labour in the ministry, and the like. Some men's profession is a snare to them. They are in reputation, and are much honoured on the account of their profession and strict walking. This often falls out in the days wherein we live, wherein all things are carried by parties. Some find themselves on the accounts mentioned, perhaps, to be the darlings and "ingentia decora," or glory of their party. If thoughts hereof secretly insinuate themselves into their hearts, and influence them into more than ordinary diligence and activity in their way and profession, they are entangled; and instead of aiming at more glory, had need lie in the dust, in a sense of their own vileness. And so close is this temptation, that oftentimes it requires no food to feed upon but that he who is entangled with it do avoid all means and ways of honour and reputation; so that it can but whisper in the heart that that avoidance is honourable. The same may be the condition with men, as was said, in preaching the gospel, in the work of the ministry. Many things in that work may yield them esteem,—their ability, their plainness, their frequency, their success; and all in this sense may be fuel unto temptations. Let, then, a man know that when he likes that which feeds his lust, and keeps it up by ways either good in themselves or not downright sinful, he is entered into temptation.

(4.) When by a man's state or condition of life, or any means whatever, it comes to pass that his lust and any temptation meet with occasions and opportunities for its provocation and stirring up, let that man know, whether he perceive it or not, that he is certainly entered into temptation. I told you before, that to enter into temptation is not merely to be tempted, but so to be under the power of it as to be entangled by it. Now, it is impossible almost for a man to have opportunities, occasions, advantages, suited to his lust and corruption, but he will be entangled. If ambassadors come from the king of Babylon, Hezekiah's pride will cast him into temptation. If Hazael be king of Syria, his cruelty and ambition will make him to rage savagely against Israel. If the priests come with their pieces of silver, Judas's covetousness will instantly be at work to sell his Master. And many instances of the like kind may, in the days wherein we live, be given. Some men think to play on the hole of the asp and not be stung, to touch pitch and not be defiled, to take fire in their clothes and not be burnt; but they will be mistaken. If thy business, course of life, societies, or whatever else it be of the like kind, do cast thee on such things, ways, persons, as suit thy lust or corruption, know that thou art entered into temptation; how thou wilt come out God only knows. Let us suppose a man that hath any seeds of filthiness in his heart engaged, in the course of his life, in society, light, vain, and foolish, what notice soever, little, great, or none at all, it be that he takes of it, he is undoubtedly entered into temptation. So is it with ambition in high places; passion in a multitude of perplexing affairs; polluted corrupt fancy in vain societies, and the perusal of idle books or treatises of vanity and folly. Fire and things combustible may more easily be induced to lie together without affecting each other, than peculiar lusts and suitable objects or occasions for their exercise.

(5.) When a man is weakened, made negligent or formal in duty, when he can omit duties or content himself with a careless, lifeless performance of them, without delight, joy, or satisfaction to his soul, who had another frame formerly; let him know, that though he may not be acquainted with the particular distemper wherein it consists, yet in something or other he is entered into temptation, which at the length he will find evident, to his trouble and peril. How many have we seen and known in our days, who, from a warm profession, have fallen to be negligent, careless, indifferent in praying, reading, hearing, and the like! Give an instance of one who hath come off without a wound, and I dare say you may find out a hundred for him that have manifested themselves to have been asleep on the top of the mast; that they were in the jaws of some vile temptation or other, that afterward brought forth bitter fruit in their lives and ways. From some few returners from folly we have every day these doleful complaints made: "Oh! I neglected private prayer; I did not meditate on the word, nor attend to hearing, but rather despised these things: and yet said I was rich and wanted nothing. Little did I consider that this unclean lust was ripening in my heart; this atheism, these abominations were fomenting there." This is a certain rule:—If his heart grow cold, negligent, or formal in duties of the worship of God, and that either as to the matter or manner of them, who hath had another frame, one temptation or other hath laid hold upon him. World, or pride, or uncleanness, or self-seeking, or malice and envy, or one thing or other, hath possessed his spirit; gray hairs are here and there upon him, though he perceive it not. And this is to be observed as to the manner of duties, as well as to the matter. Men may, upon many sinister accounts, especially for the satisfaction of their consciences, keep up and frequent duties of religion, as to the substance and matter of them, when they have no heart to them, no life in them, as to the spirituality required in their performance. Sardis kept up the performance of duties, and had therefore a name to live; but wanted spiritual life in their performances, and, was therefore "dead," Rev. iii. 1. As it is in distempers of the body, if a man find his spirits faint, his heart oppressed, his head heavy, the whole person indisposed, though he do not yet actually burn nor rave, yet he will cry, "I fear I am entering into a fever, I am so out of order and indisposed;"—a man may do so in this sickness of the soul. If he find his pulse not beat aright and evenly towards duties of worship and communion with God,—if his spirit be low, and his heart faint in them,—let him conclude, though his lust do not yet burn nor rage, that he is entered into temptation, and it is high time for him to consider the particular causes of his distemper. If the head be heavy and slumber in the things of grace, if the heart be cold in duties, evil lies at the door. And if such a soul do escape a great temptation unto sin, yet it shall not escape a great temptation by desertion. The spouse cries, "I sleep," Cant. v. 2; and that she had "put off her coat, and could not put it on;"—had an indisposition to duties and communion with Christ. What is the next news you have of her? Verse 6, Her "Beloved had withdrawn himself,"—Christ was gone; and she seeks him long and finds him not. There is such a suitableness between the new nature that is wrought and created in believers, and the duties of the worship of God, that they will not be parted nor kept asunder, unless it be by the interposition of some disturbing distemper. The new creature feeds upon them, is strengthened and increased by them, find sweetness in them, yea, meets in them with its God and Father; so that it cannot but of itself, unless made sick by some temptation, delight in them, and desire to be in the exercise of them. This frame is described in the 119th Psalm throughout. It is not, I say, cast out of this frame and temper unless it be oppressed and disordered by one secret temptation or other. Sundry other evidences there are of a soul's entering into temptation, which upon inquiry it may discover.

I propose this to take off the security that we are apt to fall into, and to manifest what is the peculiar duty that we are to apply ourselves unto in the special seasons of temptation; for he that is already entered into temptation is to apply himself unto means for disentanglement, not to labour to prevent his entering in. How this may be done I shall afterward declare.

Chapter 5

2. Having seen the danger of entering into temptation, and also discovered the ways and seasons whereby and wherein men usually so, our second inquiry is, What general directions may be given to preserve a soul from that condition that hath been spoken of? And we see our Saviour's direction in the place spoken of before, Matt. xxvi. 41. He sums up all in these two words, "Watch and pray." I shall a little labour to unfold them, and show what is inwrapped and contained in them; and that both jointly and severally:—

(1.) These is included in them a clear, abiding apprehension of great evil that there is in entering into temptation. That which a man watches and prays against, he looks upon as evil to him, and by all means to be avoided.

This, then, is the first direction:—Always bear in mind the great danger that it is for any soul to enter into temptation.

It is a woful thing to consider what slight thoughts the most have of this thing. So men can keep themselves from sin itself in open action, they are content, they scarce aim at more; on any temptation in the world, all sorts of men will venture at any time. How will young men put themselves on company, any society; at first, being delighted with evil company, then with the evil of the company! How vain are all admonitions and exhortations to them to take heed of such persons, debauched in themselves, corrupters of others, destroyers of souls! At first they will venture on the company, abhorring the thoughts of practising their lewdness; but what is the issue? Unless it be here or there one, whom God snatches with a mighty hand from the jaws of destruction, they are all lost, and become after a while in love with the evil which at first they abhorred. This open door to the ruin of souls is too evident; and woful experience makes it no less evident that it is almost impossible to fasten upon many poor creatures any fear or dread of temptation, who yet will profess a fear and abhorrency of sin. Would it were only thus with young men, such as are unaccustomed to the yoke of their Lord! What sort of men is free from this folly in one thing or other? How many professors have I known that would plead for their liberty, as they called it! They could hear any thing, all things,—all sorts of men, all men; they would try all things whether they came to them in the way of God or no; and on that account would run to hear and to attend to every broacher of false and abominable opinions, every seducer, though stigmatized by the generality of the saints: for such a one they had their liberty,—they could do it; but the opinions they hated as much as any. What hath been the issue? I scarce ever knew any come off without a wound; the most have had their faith overthrown. Let no man, then, pretend to fear sin that doth not fear temptation to it. They are too nearly allied to be separated. Satan hath put them so together that it is very hard for any man to put them asunder. He hates not the fruit who delights in the root.

When men see that such ways, such companies, such courses, such businesses, such studies and aims, do entangle them, make them cold, careless, are quench-coals to them, indispose them to even, universal, and constant obedience, if they adventure on them, sin lies at the door. It is a tender frame of spirit, sensible of its own weakness and corruption, of the craft of Satan, of the evil of sin, of the efficacy of temptation, that can perform his duty. And yet until we bring our hearts to this frame, upon the considerations before-mentioned, or the like that may be proposed, we shall never free ourselves from sinful entanglements. Boldness upon temptation, springing from several pretences, hath, as is known, ruined innumerable professors in these days, and still continues to cast many down from their excellency; nor have I the least hope of a more fruitful profession amongst us until I see more fear of temptation. Sin will not long seem great or heavy unto any to whom temptations seem light or small.

This is the first thing inwrapped in this general direction:—The daily exercise of our thoughts with an apprehension of the great danger that lies in entering into temptation, is required of us. Grief of the Spirit of God, disquietment of our own souls, loss of peace, hazard of eternal welfare, lies at the door. If the soul be not prevailed withal to the observation of this direction, all that ensues will be of no value. Temptation despised will conquer; and if the heart be made tender and watchful here, half the work of securing a good conversation is over. And let not him go any further who resolved not to improve this direction in a daily conscientious observation of it.

(2.) There is this in it also, that it is not a thing in our own power, to keep and preserve ourselves from entering into temptation. Therefore are we to pray that we may be preserved from it, because we cannot save ourselves.

This is another means of preservation. As we have no strength to resist a temptation when it doth come, when we are entered into it, but shall fall under it, without a supply of sufficiency of grace from God; so to reckon that we have no power or wisdom to keep ourselves from entering into temptation, but must be kept by the power and wisdom of God, is a preserving principle, 1 Pet. i. 5. We are in all things "kept by the power of God." This our Saviour instructs us in, not only by directing us to pray that we be not led into temptation, but also by his own praying for us, that we may be kept from it: John xvii. 15, "I pray not that thou shouldest take them out of the world, but that thou shouldest keep them from the evil,"—that is, the temptations of the world unto evil, unto sin,—ek tou ponerou, "out of evil" that is in the world, that is temptation, which is all that is evil in the world; or from the evil one, who in the world makes use of the world unto temptation. Christ prays his Father to keep us, and instructs us to pray that we be so kept. It is not, then, a thing in our own power. The ways of our entering into temptation are so many, various, and imperceptible,—the means of it so efficacious and powerful,—our weakness our unwatchfulness, so unspeakable,—that we cannot in the least keep or preserve ourselves from it. We fail both in wisdom and power for this work.

Let the heart, then commune with itself and say, "I am poor and weak; Satan is subtle, cunning, powerful, watching constantly for advantages against my soul; the world earnest, pressing, and full of specious pleas, innumerable pretences, and ways of deceit; my own corruption violent and tumultuating, enticing, entangling, conceiving sin, and warring in me, against me; occasions and advantages of temptation innumerable in all things I have done or suffer, in all businesses and persons with whom I converse; the first beginnings of temptation insensible and plausible, so that, left unto myself, I shall not know I am ensnared, until my bonds be made strong, and sin hath got ground in my heart: therefore on God alone will I rely for preservation, and continually will I look up to him on that account." This will make the soul be always committing itself to the care of God, resting itself on him, and to do nothing, undertake nothing, etc, without asking counsel of him. So that a double advantage will arise from the observation of this direction, both of singular use for the soul's preservation from the evil feared:—

1. The engagement of the grace and compassion of God, who hath called the fatherless and helpless to rest upon him; nor did ever soul fail of supplies, who, in a sense of want, rolled itself on him, on the account of his gracious invitation.

2. The keeping of it in such a frame as, on various accounts, is useful for its preservation. He that looks to God for assistance in a due manner is both sensible of his danger, and conscientiously careful in the use of means to preserve himself: which two, of what importance they are in this case, may easily be apprehended by them who have their hearts exercised in these things.

3. This also is in it,—act faith on the promise of God for preservation. To believe that he will preserve us is a means of preservation; for this God will certainly do, or make a way for us to escape out of temptation, if we fall into it under such a believing frame. We are to pray for what God hath promised. Our requests are

to be regulated by his promises and commands, which are of the same extent. Faith closes with the promises, and so finds relief in this case. This James instructs us in, chap. i. 5-7. What we want we must "ask of God;" but we must "ask in faith," for otherwise we must not "think that we shall receive any thing of the Lord." This then, also, is in this direction of our Saviour, that we act faith on the promises of God for our preservation out of temptation. He hath promised that he will keep us in all our ways; that we shall be directed in a way that, though we are fools, "we shall not err therein," Isa. xxxv. 8; that he will lead us, guide us, and deliver us from the evil one. Set faith on work on these promises of God, and expect a good and comfortable issue. It is not easily conceived what a train of graces faith is attended withal, when it goes forth to meet Christ in the promises, nor what a power for the preservation of the soul lies in this thing; but I have spoken to this elsewhere. [4]

4. Weigh these things severally, and first, take prayer into consideration. To pray that we enter not into temptation is a means to preserve us from it. Glorious things are, by all men that know aught of those things, spoken of this duty; and yet the truth is, not one half of its excellency, power, and efficacy is known. It is not my business to speak of it in general; but this I say as to my present purpose,—he that would be little in temptation, let him be much in prayer. This calls in the suitable help and succour that is laid up in Christ for us, Heb. iv. 16. This casteth our souls into a frame of opposition to every temptation. When Paul had given instruction for the taking to ourselves "the whole armour of God," that we may resist and stand in the time of temptation, he adds this general close of the whole, Eph. vi. 18, "Praying always with all prayer and supplication in the Spirit, and watching thereunto with all perseverance and supplication."

Without this all the rest will be of no efficacy for the end proposed. And therefore consider what weight he lays on it: "Praying always,"—that is, at all times and seasons, or be always ready and prepared for the discharge of that duty, Luke xviii. 1, Eph. vi. 18; "with all prayer and supplication in the Spirit,"—putting forth all kinds of desires unto God, that are suited to our condition, according to his will, lest we diverted by any thing whatever; and that not for a little while, but "with all perseverance,"—continuance lengthened out to the utmost: so shall we stand. The soul so framed is in a sure posture; and this is one of the means without which this work will not be done. If we do not abide in prayer, we shall abide in cursed temptations. Let this, then, be another direction:—Abide in prayer, and that expressly to this purpose, that we "enter not into temptation." Let this be one part of our daily contending with God,—that he would preserve our souls, and keep our hearts and our ways, that we be not entangled; that his good and wise providence will order our ways and affairs, that no pressing temptation befall us; that he would give us diligence, carefulness, and watchfulness over our own ways. So shall we be delivered when others are held with the cords of their own folly.

Chapter 6

The other part of our Saviour's direction,—namely, to "watch,"—is more general, and extends itself to many particulars. I shall fix on some things that are contained therein:

3. Watch the seasons wherein men usually do "enter into temptations."

There are sundry seasons wherein an hour of temptation is commonly at hand, and will unavoidably seize upon the soul, unless it be delivered by mercy in the use of watchfulness. When we are under such a season, then are we peculiarly to be upon our guard that we enter not into, that we fall not under, the power of temptation. Some of those seasons may be named:—

(1.) A season of unusual outward prosperity is usually accompanied with an hour of temptation. Prosperity and temptation go together; yea, prosperity is a temptation, many temptations, and that because, without eminent supplies of grace, it is apt to cast a soul into a frame and temper exposed to any temptation, and provides it with fuel and food for all. It hath provision for lust and darts for Satan.

The wise man tells us that the "prosperity of fools destroys them," Prov. i. 32. It hardens them in their way, makes them despise instruction, and put the evil day (whose terror should influence them into amendment) far from them. Without a special assistance, it hath an inconceivably malignant influence on believers themselves. Hence Agur prays against riches, because of the temptation that attends them: "Lest," saith he, "I be full and deny thee, and say, Who is the Lord?" Prov. xxx. 8, 9;—lest, being filled with them, he should forget the Lord; as God complains that his people did, Hos. xiii. 6.

We know how David was mistaken in this case: Ps. xxx. 6, "I said in my prosperity, I shall never be moved." All is well, and will be well. But what was at hand, what lay at the door, that David thought not of? Verse 7, "Thou didst hide thy face, and I was troubled." God was ready to hide his face, and David to enter into a temptation of desertion, and he knew it not.

As, then, unto a prosperous condition. I shall not run cross to Solomon's counsel, "In the day of prosperity rejoice," Eccles. vii. 14. Rejoice in the God of thy mercies, who doth thee good in his patience and forbearance, notwithstanding all thy unworthiness. Yet I may add to it, from the same fountain of wisdom, "Consider," also, lest evil lie at the door. A man in that state is in the midst of snares. Satan hath many advantages against him; he forgeth darts out of all his enjoyments; and, if he watch not, he will be entangled before he is aware.

Thou wantest that which should poise and ballast thy heart. Formality in religion will be apt to creep upon thee; and that lays the soul open to all temptations in their full power and strength. Satisfaction and delight in creature-comforts, the poison of the soul, will be apt to grow upon thee. In such a time be vigilant, be circumspect, or thou wilt be surprised. Job says, that in his affliction "God made his heart soft," chap. xxiii. 16. There is a hardness, an insensible want of spiritual sense, gathered in prosperity, that, if not watched against, will expose the heart to the deceits of sin and baits of Satan. "Watch and pray" in this season. Many men's negligence in it hath cost them dear; their woful experience cries out to take heed. Blessed is he that feareth always, but especially in a time of prosperity.

(2.) As in part was manifested before, a time of the slumber of grace, of neglect in communion with God, of formality in duty, is a season to be watched in, as that which certainly some other temptation attending it.

Let a soul in such an estate awake and look about him. His enemy is at hand, and he is ready to fall into such a condition as may cost him dear all the days of his life. His present estate is bad enough in itself; but it is an indication of that which is worse that lies at the door. The disciples that were with Christ in the mount had not only a bodily, but a spiritual drowsiness upon them. What says our Saviour to them? "Arise; watch and pray, that ye enter not into temptation." We know how near one of them was to a bitter hour of temptation, and not watching as he ought, he immediately entered into it.

I mentioned before the case of the spouse, Cant. v. 2-8. She slept, and was drowsy, and unwilling to gird up herself to a vigorous performance of duties, in a way of quick, active communion with Christ. Before she is aware, she hath lost her Beloved; then she moans, inquires, cries, endures woundings, reproaches, and all, before she obtains him again. Consider, then, O poor soul, thy state and condition! Doth thy light burn dim? or though it give to others as great a blaze as formerly, yet thou seest not so clearly the face of God in Christ by it as thou hast done? 2 Cor. iv. 6. Is thy zeal cold? or if it do the same works as formerly, yet thy heart is not warmed with the love of God and to God in them as formerly, but only thou proceedest in the course thou hast been in? Art thou negligent in the duties of praying or hearing? or if thou dost observe them, thou doest it not with that life and vigour as formerly? Dost thou flag in thy profession? or if thou keep it up, yet thy wheels are oiled by some sinister respects from within or without? Does thy delight in the people of God faint and grow cold? or is thy love to them changing from that which is purely spiritual into that which is very carnal, upon the account of suitableness of principles and natural spirits, if not worse foundations? If thou art drowsing in such a condition as this, take heed; thou art falling into some woful temptation that will break all thy bones, and give thee wounds that shall stick by thee all the days of thy life. Yea, when thou awakest, thou wilt find that it hath indeed laid hold of thee already, though thou perceivedst it not; it hath smitten and wounded thee, though thou hast not complained nor sought for relief or healing.

Such was the state of the church of Sardis, Rev. iii. 2. "The things that remained were ready to die." "Be watchful," says our Saviour, "and strengthen them, or a worse thing will befall thee." If any that reads the word of this direction be in this condition, if he hath any regard of his poor soul, let him now awake, before he be entangled beyond recovery. Take this warning from God; despise it not.

(3.) A season of great spiritual enjoyments is often, by the malice of Satan and the weakness of our hearts, turned into a season of danger as to this business of temptation.

We know how the case stood with Paul, 2 Cor. xii. 7. He had glorious spiritual revelations of God and Jesus Christ. Instantly Satan falls upon him, a messenger from him buffets him; so that he earnestly begs its departure, but yet is left to struggle with it. God is pleased sometimes to give us especial discoveries of himself and his love, to fill the heart with his kindness; Christ takes us into the banqueting-house, and gives our hearts their fills of love; and this by some signal work of his Spirit, overpowering us with a sense of love in the unspeakable privilege of adoption, and so fills our souls with joy unspeakable and glorious. A man would think this was the securest condition in the world. What soul does not cry with Peter in the mount, "It is good for me to be here; to abide here for ever?" But yet very frequently some bitter temptation is now at hand. Satan sees that, being possessed by the joy before us, we quickly neglect many ways of approach to our souls, wherein he seeks and finds advantages against us. Is this, then, our state and condition? Does God at any time give us to drink of the rivers of pleasure that are at his right hand, and satisfy our souls with his kindness as with marrow and fatness? Let us not say, "We shall never be moved;" we know not how soon God may hide his face, or a messenger from Satan may buffet us.

Besides, there lies oftentimes a greater and worse deceit in this business. Men cheat their souls with their own fancies, instead of a sense of God's love by the Holy Ghost; and when they are lifted up with their imaginations, it is not expressible how fearfully they are exposed to all manner of temptations;—and how, then, are they able to find relief against their consciences from their own foolish fancies and deceivings, wherewith they sport themselves? May we not see such every day,—persons walking in the vanities and ways of this world, yet boasting of their sense of the love of God? Shall we believe them? We must not, then, believe truth itself; and how woful, then, must their condition needs be!

(4.) A fourth season is a season of self-confidence; then usually temptation is at hand.

The case of Peter is clear unto this. "I will not deny thee; though all men should deny thee I will not; though I were to die for it, I would not do it." This said the poor man when he stood on the very brink of that temptation that cost him in the issue such bitter tears. And this taught him so far to know himself all his days, and gave him such acquaintance with the state of all believers, that when he had received more of the Spirit and of power, yet he had less of confidence, and saw it was fit that others should have so also, and therefore persuades all men to "pass the time of their sojourning here in fear," 1 Pet. i. 17; not to be confident and high as he was, lest, as he did, they fall. At the first trial he compares himself with others, and vaunts himself above them: "Though all men should forsake thee, yet I will not." He fears every man more than himself. But when our Saviour afterward comes to him, and puts him directly upon the comparison, "Simon, son of Jonas, lovest thou me more than these?" John xxi. 15, he hath done comparing himself with others, and only crieth, "Lord, thou knowest that I love thee." He will lift up himself above others no more. Such a season oftentimes falls out. Temptations are abroad in the world, false doctrines, with innumerable other allurements and provocations: we are ready every one to be very confident that we shall not be surprised with them: though all men should fall into these follies yet we would not: surely we shall never go off from our walking with God; it is impossible our hearts should be so sottish. But says the apostle, "Be not high-minded, but fear; let him that thinketh he standeth take heed lest he fall." Wouldst thou think that Peter, who had walked on the sea with Christ, confessed him to be the Son of God, been with him in the mount, when he heard the voice from the excellent glory, should, at the word of a servant-girl, when there was no legal inquisition after him no process against him nor any one in his condition, instantly fall a-cursing and swearing that he knew him not? Let them take heed of self-confidence who have any mind to take heed of sin. And this is the first thing in our watching, to consider well the seasons wherein temptation usually makes its approaches to the soul, and be armed against them. And these are some of the seasons wherein temptations are nigh at hand.

Chapter 7

That part of watchfulness against temptation which we have considered regards the outward means, occasions, and advantages of temptation; proceed we now to that which respects the heart itself, which is wrought upon and entangled by temptation. Watching or keeping of the heart, which above all keepings we are obliged unto, comes within the compass of this duty also; for the right performance whereof take these ensuing directions:—

(1.) Let him that would not enter into temptations labour to know his own heart, to be acquainted with his own spirit, his natural frame and temper, his lusts and corruptions, his natural, sinful, or spiritual weaknesses, that, finding where his weakness lies, he may be careful to keep at a distance from all occasions of sin.

Our Saviour tells the disciples that "they knew not what spirit they were of;" which, under a pretence of zeal, betrayed them into ambition and desire of revenge. Had they known it they would have watched over themselves. David tells us, Ps. xviii. 23, that he considered his ways, and "kept himself from his iniquity," which he was particularly prone unto.

There are advantages for temptations lying oftentimes in men's natural tempers and constitutions. Some are naturally gentle, facile, easy to be entreated, pliable; which, though it be the noblest temper of nature, and the best and choicest ground, when well broken up and fallowed for grace to grow in, yet, if not watched over, will be a means of innumerable surprisals and entanglements in temptation. Others are earthy, froward, morose; so that envy, malice, selfishness, peevishness, harsh thoughts of other, repinings, lie at the very door of their natures, and they can scarce step out but they are in the snare of one or other of them. Others are passionate, and the like. Now, he that would watch that he enter not into temptation, had need be acquainted with his own natural temper, that he may watch over the treacheries that lie in it continually. Take heed lest you have a Jehu in you, that shall make you drive furiously; or a Jonah in you, that will make you ready to repine; or a David, that will make you hasty in your determinations, as he was often, in the warmth and goodness of his natural temper. He who watches not this thoroughly, who is not exactly skilled in the knowledge of himself, will never be disentangled from one temptation or another all his days.

Again: as men have peculiar natural tempers, which, according as they are attended or managed, prove a great fomes of sin, or advantage to the exercise of grace; so men may have peculiar lusts or corruptions, which, either by their natural constitution or education, and other prejudices, have got deep rooting and strength in them. This, also, is to be found out by him who would not enter into temptation. Unless he know it, unless his eyes be always on it, unless he observes its actings, motions, advantages, it will continually be entangling and ensnaring of him. This, then, is our sixth direction in this kind:—Labour to know thine own frame and temper; what spirit thou art of; what associates in thy heart Satan hath; where corruption is strong, where grace is weak; what stronghold lust hath in thy natural constitution, and the like. How many have all their comforts blasted and peace disturbed by their natural passion and peevishness! How many are rendered useless in the world by their frowardness and discontent! How many are disquieted even by their own gentleness and facility! Be acquainted, then, with thine own heart: though it be deep, search it; though it be dark, inquire into it; though it give all its distempers other names than what are their due, believe it not. Were not men utter strangers to themselves,—did they not give flattering titles to their natural distempers,—did they not strive rather to justify, palliate, or excuse the evils of their hearts, that are suited to their natural tempers and constitutions, than to destroy them, and by these means keep themselves off from taking a clear and distinct view of them,—it were impossible that they should all their days hang in the same briers without attempt for deliverance. Uselessness and scandal in professors are branches growing constantly on this root of unacquaintedness with their own frame and temper; and how few are there who will either study them themselves or bear with those who would acquaint them with them!

(2.) When thou knowest the state and condition of thy heart as to the particulars mentioned, watch against all such occasions and opportunities, employments, societies, retirements, businesses, as are apt to entangle thy natural temper or provoke thy corruption.

It may be there are some ways, some societies, some businesses, that thou never in thy life escapedst them, but sufferedst by them more or less, through their suitableness to entice or provoke thy corruption; it may be thou art in a state and condition of life that weary thee day by day, on the account of thy ambition, passion, discontent, or the like: if thou hast any love to thy soul, it is time for thee to awake and to deliver thyself as a bird from the evil snare. Peter will not come again in haste to the high priest's hall; nor would David walk again on the top of his house, when he should have been on the high places of the field. But the particulars of this instance are so various, and of such several natures in respect of several persons, that it is impossible to enumerate them, Prov. iv. 14, 15. Herein lies no small part of that wisdom which consists in our ordering our conversation aright. Seeing we have so little power over our hearts when once they meet with suitable provocations, we are to keep them asunder, as a man would do fire and the combustible parts of the house wherein he dwells.

(3.) Be sure to lay in provision in store against the approaching of any temptation.

This also belongs to our watchfulness over our hearts. You will say, "What provision is intended, and where is it to be laid up?" Our hearts, as our Saviour speaks, are our treasury. There we lay up whatever we have, good or bad; and thence do we draw it for our use,
whatever we have, good or bad; and thence do we draw it for our use,
Matt. xii. 35. It is the heart, then, wherein provision is to be laid up

against temptation. When an enemy draws nigh to a fort or castle to besiege and take it, oftentimes, if he find it well manned and furnished with provision for a siege, and so able to hold out, he withdraws and assaults it not. If Satan, the prince of this world, come and find our hearts fortified against his batteries, and provided to hold out, he not only departs, but, as James says, he flees: "He will flee from us," James iv. 7. For the provision to be laid up, it is that which is provided in the gospel for us. Gospel provisions will do this work; that is, keep the heart full of a sense of the love of God in Christ. This is the greatest preservative against the power of temptation in the world. Joseph had this; and therefore, on the first appearance of temptation, he cries out, "How can I do this great evil, and sin against God?" and there is an end of the temptation as to him; it lays no hold on him, but departs. He was furnished with such a ready sense of the love of God as temptation could not stand before, Gen. xxxix. 9. "The love of Christ constraineth us," saith the apostle, "to live to him," 2 Cor. v. 14; and so, consequently, to withstand temptation. A man may, nay, he ought to lay in provisions of the law also,—fear of death, hell, punishment, with the terror of the Lord in them. But these are far more easily conquered than the other; nay, they will never stand alone against a vigorous assault. They are conquered in convinced persons every day; hearts stored with them will struggle for a while, but quickly give over. But store the heart with a sense of the love of God in Christ, and his love in the shedding of it; get a relish of the privileges we have thereby,—our adoption, justification, acceptation with God; fill the heart with thoughts of the beauty of his death;—and thou wilt, in an ordinary course of walking with God, have great peace and security as to the disturbance of temptations. When men can live and plod on in their profession, and not be able to say when they had any living sense of the love of God or of the privileges which we have in the blood of Christ, I know not what they can have to keep them from falling into snares. The apostle tells us that the "peace of God," phrouresei tas kardias, Phil. iv. 7 "shall keep our hearts." Phroura denotes a military word,—a garrison; and so phrouresei is, "shall keep as in a garrison." Now, a garrison hath two things attending it,—first, That it is exposed to the assaults of its enemies; secondly, That safety lies in it from their attempts. It is so with our souls; they are exposed to temptations, assaulted continually; but if there be a garrison in them, or if they be kept as in a garrison, temptation shall not enter, and consequently we shall not enter into temptation. Now, how is this done? Saith he, "The peace of God shall do it." What is this "peace of God?" A sense of his love and favour in Jesus Christ. Let this abide in you, and it shall garrison you against all assaults whatever. Besides, there is that, in an especial manner, which is also in all the rest of the directions,—namely, that the thing itself lies in a direct opposition to all the ways and means that temptation can make use of to approach unto our souls. Contending to obtain and keep a sense of the love of God in Christ, in the nature of it, obviates all the workings and insinuations of temptation. Let this be a third direction, then, in our watching against temptation:—Lay in store of gospel provisions, that may make the soul a defenced place against all the assaults thereof.

(4.) In the first approach of any temptation, as we are all tempted, these directions following are also suited to carry on the work of watching, which we are in the pursuit of:—

1. Be always awake, that thou mayst have an early discovery of thy temptation, that thou mayst know it so to be. Most men perceive not their enemy until they are wounded by him. Yea, others may sometimes see them deeply engaged, whilst themselves are utterly insensible; they sleep without any sense of danger, until others come and awake them by telling them that their house is on fire. Temptation in a neuter sense is not easily discoverable,—namely, as it denotes such a way, or thing, or matter, as is or may be made use of for the ends of temptation. Few take notice of it until it is too late, and they find themselves entangled, if not wounded. Watch, then, to understand betimes the snares that are laid for thee,—to understand the advantages thy enemies have against thee, before they get

strength and power, before they are incorporated with thy lusts, and have distilled poison into thy soul.

2. Consider the aim and tendency of the temptation, whatever it be, and of all that are concerned in it. Those who have an active concurrence into thy temptation are Satan and thy own lusts. For thine own lust, I have manifested elsewhere what it aims at in all its actings and enticings. It never rises up but its intendment is the worst of evils. Every acting of it would be a formed enmity against God. Hence look upon it in its first attempts, what pretences soever may be made, as thy mortal enemy. "I hate it," saith the apostle, Rom. vii. 15,—that is, the working of lust in me. "I hate it; it is the greatest enemy I have. Oh, that it were killed and destroyed! Oh, that I were delivered out of the power of it!" Know, then, that in the first attempt or assault in any temptation, the most cursed, sworn enemy is at hand, is setting on thee, and that for thy utter ruin; so that it were the greatest madness in the world to throw thyself into his arms to be destroyed. But of this I have spoken in my discourse of Mortification.

Hath Satan any more friendly aim and intention towards thee, who is a sharer in every temptation? To beguile thee as a serpent, to devour thee as a lion, is the friendship that he owes thee. I shall only add, that the sin he tempts thee to against the law, it is not the thing he aims at; his design lies against thy interest in the gospel. He would make sin but a bridge to get over to a better ground, to assault thee as to thy interest in Christ. He who perhaps will say today, "Thou mayst venture on sin, because thou hast an interest in Christ," will tomorrow tell thee to the purpose that thou hast none, because thou hast done so.

3. Meet thy temptation in its entrance with thoughts of faith concerning Christ on the cross; this will make it sink before thee. Entertain no parley, no dispute with it, if thou wouldst not enter into it. Say, "?It is Christ that died,'—that died for such sins as these." This is called "taking the shield of faith to quench the fiery darts of Satan," Eph. vi. 16. Faith doth it by laying hold on Christ crucified,

his love therein, and what from thence he suffered for sin. Let thy temptation be what it will,—be it unto sin, to fear or doubting for sin, or about thy state and condition,—it is not able to stand before faith lifting up the standard of the cross. We know what means the Papists, who have lost the power of faith, use to keep up the form. They will sign themselves with the sign of the cross, or make aerial crosses; and by virtue of that work done, think to scare away the devil. To act faith on Christ crucified is really to sign ourselves with the sign of the cross, and thereby shall we overcome that wicked one, 1 Pet. v. 9.

4. Suppose the soul hath been surprised by temptation, and entangled at unawares, so that now it is too late to resist the first entrances of it, what shall such a soul do that it be not plunged into it, and carried away with the power thereof?

1st. Do as Paul did: beseech God again and again that it may "depart from thee," 2 Cor. xii. 8. And if thou abidest therein, thou shalt certainly either be speedily delivered out of it, or receive a sufficiency of grace not to be foiled utterly by it. Only, as I said in part before, do not so much employ thy thoughts about the things whereunto thou art tempted, which oftentimes raiseth farther entanglements, but set thyself against the temptation itself. Pray against the temptation that it may depart; and when that is taken away, the things themselves may be more calmly considered.

2dly. Fly to Christ, in a peculiar manner, as he was tempted, and beg of him to give thee succour in this "needful time of trouble." Heb. iv. 16, the apostle instructs us herein: "In that he hath been tempted, he is able to succour them that are tempted." This is the meaning of it: "When you are tempted and are ready to faint, when you want succour,—you must have it or you die,—act faith peculiarly on Christ as he was tempted; that is, consider that he was tempted himself,—that he suffered thereby,—that he conquered all temptations, and that not merely on his own account, seeing for our sakes he submitted to be tempted, but for us," (he conquered in and by himself, but for us.) And draw, yea, expect succour from him, Heb. iv. 15, 16. Lie down at his feet, make thy complaint known to him, beg his assistance, and it will not be in vain.

3dly. Look to Him who hath promised deliverancc. Consider that he is faithful, and will not suffer thee to be tempted above what thou art able. Consider that he hath promised a comfortable issue of these trials and temptations. Call all the promises to mind of assistance and deliverance that he hath made; ponder them in thy heart. And rest upon it, that God hath innumerable ways that thou knowest not of to give thee in deliverance; as,—

(1st.) He can send an affliction that shall mortify thy heart unto the matter of the temptation, whatever it be, that that which was before a sweet morsel under the tongue shall neither have taste or relish in it unto thee,—thy desire to it shall be killed; as was the case with David: or,

(2dly.) He can, by some providence, alter that whole state of things from whence thy temptation doth arise, so taking fuel from the fire, causing it to go out of itself; as it was with the same David in the day of battle: or,

(3dly.) He can tread down Satan under thy feet, that he shall not dare to suggest any thing any more to thy disadvantage (the God of peace shall do it), that thou shalt hear of him no more: or,

(4thly.) He can give thee such supply of grace as that thou mayst be freed, though not from the temptation itself, yet from the tendency and danger of it; as was the case with Paul: or,

(5thly.) He can give thee such a comfortable persuasion of good success in the issue as that thou shalt have refreshment in thy trials, and be kept from the trouble of the temptation; as was thc case with the same Paul: or,

(6thly.) He can utterly remove it, and make thee a complete conqueror. And innumerable other ways he hath of keeping thee from entering into temptation, so as to be foiled by it.

4thly. Consider where the temptation wherewith thou art surprised hath made its entrance, and by what means, and with all speed make up the breach. Stop that passage which the waters have made to enter in at. Deal with thy soul like a wise physician. Inquire when, how, by what means, thou fellest into this distemper; and if thou findest negligence, carelessness, want of keeping watch over thyself, to have lain at the bottom of it, fix thy soul there,—bewail that before the Lord,—make up that breach,—and then proceed to the work that lies before thee.

Chapter 8

The directions insisted on in the former chapters are such as are partly given us, in their several particulars, up and down the Scripture; partly arise from the nature of the thing itself. There is one general direction remains, which is comprehensive of all that went before, and also adds many more particulars unto them. This contains an approved antidote against the poison of temptation,—a remedy that Christ himself hath marked with a note of efficacy and success; that is given us, Rev. iii. 10, in the words of our Saviour himself to the church of Philadelphia. "Because," saith he, "thou hast kept the word of my patience, I will also keep thee from the hour of temptation, which shall come upon all the world, to try them that dwell in the earth." Christ is "the same yesterday, today, and for ever." As he dealt with the church of Philadelphia, so will he deal with us. If we "keep the word of his patience," he will "keep us from the hour of temptation." This, then, being a way of rolling the whole care of this weighty affair on him who is able to bear it, it requires our peculiar attention.

And, therefore, I shall show,—

(1.) What it is to "keep the word of Christ's patience," that we may know how to perform our duty; and,

(2.) How this will be a means of our preservation, which will establish us in the faith of Christ's promise.

(1.) The word of Christ is the word of the gospel; the word by him revealed from the bosom of the Father; the word of the Word; the word spoken in time of the eternal Word. So it is called "The word of Christ," Col. iii. 16; or "The gospel of Christ," Rom. i. 16, 1 Cor. ix.

12; and "The doctrine of Christ," Heb. vi. 1. "Of Christ," that is, as its author, Heb. i. 1, 2; and of him, as the chief subject or matter of it, 2 Cor. i. 20. Now, this word is called "The word of Christ's patience," or tolerance and forbearance, upon the account of that patience and long-suffering which, in the dispensation of it, the Lord Christ exerciseth towards the whole, and to all persons in it; and that both actively and passively, in his bearing with men and enduring from them:—

1. He is patient towards his saints; he bears with them, suffers from them. He is "patient to us-ward," 2 Pet. iii. 9,—that is, that believe. The gospel is the word of Christ's patience even to believers. A soul acquainted with the gospel knows that there is no property of Christ rendered more glorious therein than that of his patience. That he should bear with so many unkindnesses, so many causeless breaches, so many neglects of his love, so many affronts done to his grace, so many violations of engagements as he doth, it manifests his gospel to be not only the word of his grace, but also of his patience. He suffers also from them in all the reproaches they bring upon his name and ways; and he suffers in them, for "in all their afflictions he is afflicted."

2. Towards the elect not yet effectually called. Rev. iii. 20, he stands waiting at the door of their hearts and knocks for an entrance. He deals with them by all means, and yet stands and waits until "his head is filled with the dew, and his locks with the drops of the night," Cant. v. 2; as enduring the cold and inconveniences of the night, that when his morning is come he may have entrance. Oftentimes for a long season he is by them scorned in his person, persecuted in his saints and ways, reviled in his word, whilst he stands at the door in the word of his patience, with his heart full of love towards their poor rebellious souls.

3. To the perishing world. Hence the time of his kingdom in this world is called the time of his "patience," Rev. i. 9. He "endures the

vessels of wrath with much long-suffering," Rom. ix. 22. Whilst the gospel is administered in the world he is patient towards the men thereof, until the saints in heaven and earth are astonished and cry out, "How long?" Ps. xiii. 1, 2; Rev. vi. 10. And themselves do mock at him as if he were an idol, 2 Pet. iii. 4. He endures from them bitter things, in his name, ways, worship, saints, promises, threats, all his interest of honour and love; and yet passeth by them, lets them alone, does them good. Nor will he cut this way of proceeding short until the gospel shall be preached no more. Patience must accompany the gospel.

Now, this is the word that is to be kept, that we may be kept from "the hour of temptation."

(2.) Three things are implied in the keeping of this word:

1. Knowledge;
2. Valuation;
3. Obedience:—

1. Knowledge. He that will keep this word must know it, be acquainted with it, under a fourfold notion:—

1st. As a word of grace and mercy, to save him;

2dly. As a word of holiness and purity, to sanctify him;

3dly. As a word of liberty and power, to ennoble him and set him free;

4thly. As a word of consolation, to support him in every condition:—

1st. As a word of grace and mercy, able to save us: "It is the power of God unto salvation," Rom. i. 16; "The grace of God that bringeth forth salvation," Tit. ii. 11; "The word of grace that is able to build us up, and to give us an inheritance among all them that are sanctified," Acts xx. 32; "The word that is able to save our souls," James i. 21. When the word of the gospel is known as a word of mercy, grace, and pardon, as the sole evidence for life, as the conveyance of an eternal inheritance; when the soul finds it such to itself, it will strive to keep it.

2dly. As a word of holiness and purity, able to sanctify him: "Ye are clean through the word I have spoken unto you," saith our Saviour, John xv. 3. To that purpose is his prayer, chap. xvii. 17. He that knows not the word of Christ's patience as a sanctifying, cleansing word, in the power of it upon his own soul, neither knows it nor keeps it. The empty profession of our days knows not one step towards this duty; and thence it is that the most are so overborne under the power of temptations. Men full of self, of the world, of fury, ambition, and almost all unclean lusts, do yet talk of keeping the word of Christ! See 1 Pet. i. 2; 2 Tim. ii. 19.

3dly. As a word of liberty and power, to ennoble him and set him free;—and this not only from the guilt of sin and from wrath, for that it doth as it is a word of grace and mercy; not only from the power of sin, for that it doth as it is a word of holiness; but also from all outward respects of men or the world that might entangle him or enslave him. It declares us to be "Christ's freemen," and in bondage unto none, John viii. 32; 1 Cor. vii. 23. We are not by it freed from due subjection unto superiors, nor from any duty, nor unto any sin, 1 Pet. ii. 16; but in two respects it is a word of freedom, liberty, largeness of mind, power and deliverance from bondage:—

(1st.) In respect of conscience as to the worship of God, Gal. v. 1.

(2dly.) In respect of ignoble, slavish respects unto the men or things of the world, in the course of our pilgrimage. The gospel gives a free, large, and noble spirit, in subjection to God, and none else. There is administered in it a spirit "not of fear, but of power, and of love, and of a sound mind," 2 Tim. i. 7; a mind "in nothing terrified," Phil. i. 28,—not swayed with any by-respect whatever. There is nothing more unworthy of the gospel than a mind in bondage to persons or things, prostituting itself to the lusts of men or affrightments of the world. And he that thus knows the word of Christ's patience, really and in power, is even thereby freed from innumerable, from unspeakable temptations.

4thly. As a word of consolation, to support him in every condition, and to be a full portion in the want of all. It is a word attended with "joy unspeakable and full of glory." It gives supportment, relief, refreshment, satisfaction, peace, consolation, joy, boasting, glory, in every condition whatever. Thus to know the word of Christ's patience, thus to know the gospel, is the first part, and it is a great part, of this condition of our preservation from the hour and power of temptation.

2. Valuation of what is thus known belongs to the keeping of this word. It is to be kept as a treasure. 2 Tim. i. 14, Ten kalen parakatatheken,—that excellent "depositum" (that is, the word of the gospel),—"keep it," saith the apostle, "by the Holy Ghost;" and, "Hold fast the faithful word," Tit. i. 9. It is a good treasure, a faithful word; hold it fast. It is a word that comprises the whole interest of Christ in the world. To value that as our chiefest treasure is to keep the word of Christ's patience. They that will have a regard from Christ in the time of temptation are not to be regardless of his concernments.

3. Obedience. Personal obedience, in the universal observation of all the commands of Christ, is the keeping of his word, John xiv. 15. Close adherence unto Christ in holiness and universal obedience, then when the opposition that the gospel of Christ doth meet withal in the world doth render it signally the word of his patience, is the life and soul of the duty required.

Now, all these are to be so managed with that intension of mind and spirit, that care of heart and diligence of the whole person, as to make up a keeping of this word; which evidently includes all these considerations.

We are arrived, then, to the sum of this safeguarding duty, of this condition of freedom from the power of temptation:—He that, having a due acquaintance with the gospel in its excellencies, as to him a word of mercy, holiness, liberty, and consolation, values it, in all its concernments, as his choicest and only treasure,—makes it his business and the work of his life to give himself up unto it in universal obedience, then especially when opposition and apostasy put the patience of Christ to the utmost,—he shall be preserved from the hour of temptation.

This is that which is comprehensive of all that went before, and is exclusive of all other ways for the obtaining of the end purposed. Nor let any man think without this to be kept one hour from entering into temptation; wherever he fails, there temptation enters. That this will be a sure preservative may appear from the ensuing considerations:—

(1.) It hath the promise of preservation, and this alone hath so. It is solemnly promised, in the place mentioned, to the church of Philadelphia on this account. When a great trial and temptation was to come on the world, at the opening of the seventh seal, Rev. vii. 3, a caution is given for the preservation of God's sealed ones, which are described to be those who keep the word of Christ; for the promise is that it should be so.

Now, in every promise there are three things to be considered:—

1. The faithfulness of the Father, who gives it. [2.] The grace of the Son, which is the matter of it. [3.] The power and efficacy of the Holy Ghost, which puts the promise in execution. And all these are engaged for the preservation of such persons from the hour of temptation.

1. The faithfulness of God accompanieth the promise. On this account is our deliverance laid, 1 Cor. x. 13. Though we be tempted, yet we shall be kept from the hour of temptation; it shall not grow too strong for us. What comes on us we shall be able to bear; and what would be too hard for us we shall escape. But what security have we hereof? Even the faithfulness of God: "God is faithful, who will not suffer you," etc. And wherein is God's faithfulness seen and exercised? "He is faithful that promised," Heb. x. 23; his faithfulness consists in his discharge of his promises. "He abideth faithful: he cannot deny himself," 2 Tim. ii. 13. So that by being under the promise, we have the faithfulness of God engaged for our preservation.

2. There is in every promise of the covenant the grace of the Son; that is the subject-matter of all promises: "I will keep thee." How? "By my grace with thee." So that what assistance the grace of Christ can give a soul that hath a right in this promise, in the hour of temptation it shall enjoy it. Paul's temptation grew very high; it was likely to have come to its prevalent hour. He "besought the Lord, that is, the Lord Jesus Christ, for help, 2 Cor. xii. 8; and received that answer from him, "My grace is sufficient for thee," verse 9. That it was the Lord Christ and his grace with whom he had peculiarly to do is evident from the close of that verse: "I will glory in my infirmity, that the power of Christ may rest upon me;" or "the efficacy of the grace of Christ in my preservation be made evident." So Heb. ii. 18.

3. The efficacy of the Spirit accompanieth the promises. He is called "The Holy Spirit of promise;" not only because he is promised by Christ, but also because he effectually makes good the promise, and gives it accomplishment in our souls. He also, then, is engaged to preserve the soul walking according to the rule laid down. See Isa. lix. 21. Thus, where the promise is, there is all this assistance. The faithfulness of the Father, the grace of the Son, the power of the Spirit, all are engaged in our preservation.

(2.) This constant, universal keeping of Christ's word of patience will keep the heart and soul in such a frame, as wherein no prevalent temptation, by virtue of any advantages whatever, can seize upon it, so as totally to prevail against it. So David prays, Ps. xxv. 21, "Let integrity and uprightness preserve me." This integrity and uprightness is the Old Testament keeping the word of Christ,—universal close walking with God. Now, how can they preserve a man? Why, by keeping his heart in such a frame, so defended on every side, that no evil can approach or take hold on him. Fail a man in his integrity, he hath an open place for temptation to enter, Isa. lvii. 21. To keep the word of Christ, is to do this universally, as hath been showed. This exercises grace in all the faculties of the soul, and compasses it with the whole armour of God. The understanding is full of light; the affections, of love and holiness. Let the wind blow from what quarter it will, the soul is fenced and fortified; let the enemy assault when or by what means he pleaseth, all things in the soul of such a one are upon the guard; "How can I do this thing, and sin against God?" is at hand. Especially, upon a twofold account doth deliverance and security arise from his hand:—

1. By the mortification of the heart unto the matter of temptations. The prevalency of any temptation arises from hence, that the heart is ready to close with the matter of it. There are lusts within, suited to the proposals of the world or Satan without. Hence James resolves all temptations into our "own lusts," chap. i. 14; because either they proceed from or are made effectual by them, as hath been declared. Why doth terror or threats turn us aside from a due constancy in the performance of our duty? Is it not because there is unmortified, carnal fear abiding in us, that tumultuates in such a season? Why is it that the allurements of the world and compliances with men entangle us? Is it not because our affections are entangled with the things and considerations proposed unto us? Now, keeping the word of Christ's patience, in the manner declared, keeps the heart mortified to these things, and so it is not easily entangled by them. Saith the apostle, Gal. ii. 20, "I am crucified with Christ." He that keeps close to Christ

is crucified with him, and is dead to all the desires of the flesh and the world; as more fully, chap. vi. 14. Here the match is broken, and all love, entangling love, dissolved. The heart is crucified to the world and all things in it. Now the matter of all temptations almost is taken out of the world; the men of it, or the things of it, make them up. "As to these things," says the apostle, "I am crucified to them," (and it is so with every one that keeps the word of Christ.) "My heart is mortified unto them. I have no desire after them, nor affection to them, nor delight in them, and they are crucified unto me. The crowns, glories, thrones, pleasures, profits of the world, I see nothing desirable in them. The reputation among them, they are all as a thing of nought. I have no value nor estimation of them." When Achan saw the "goodly Babylonian garment, and two hundred shekels of silver, and a wedge of gold," first he "coveted them," then he "took them," Josh. vii. 21. Temptation subtly spreads the Babylonish garment of favour, praise, peace, the silver of pleasure or profit, with the golden contentments of the flesh, before the eyes of men. If now there be that in them alive, unmortified, that will presently fall a-coveting; let what fear of punishment will ensue, the heart of hand will be put forth into iniquity.

Herein, then, lies the security of such a frame as that described: It is always accompanied with a mortified heart, crucified unto the things that are the matter of our temptations; without which it is utterly impossible that we should be preserved one moment when any temptation doth befall us. If liking, and love of the things proposed, insinuated, commended in the temptation, be living and active in us, we shall not be able to resist and stand.

2. In this frame the heart is filled with better things and their excellency, so far as to be fortified against the matter of any temptation. See what resolution this puts Paul upon, Phil. iii. 8; all is "loss and dung" to him. Who would go out of his way to have his arms full of loss and dung? And whence is it that he hath this estimation of the most desirable things in the world? It is from that dear estimation he had of the excellency of Christ. So, verse 10,

when the soul is exercised to communion with Christ, and to walking with him, he drinks new wine, and cannot desire the old things of the world, for he says "The new is better." He tastes every day how gracious the Lord is; and therefore longs not after the sweetness of forbidden things,—which indeed have none. He that makes it his business to eat daily of the tree of life will have no appetite unto other fruit, though the tree that bear them seem to stand in the midst of paradise. This the spouse makes the means of her preservation; even the excellency which, by daily communion, she found in Christ and his graces above all other desirable things. Let a soul exercise itself to a communion with Christ in the good things of the gospel,—pardon of sin, fruits of holiness, hope of glory, peace with God, joy in the Holy Ghost, dominion over sin,—and he shall have a mighty preservative against all temptations. As the full soul loatheth the honey-comb,—as a soul filled with carnal, earthly, sensual contentments finds no relish nor savour in the sweetest spiritual things; so he that is satisfied with the kindness of God, as with marrow and fatness,—that is, every day entertained at the banquet of wine, wine upon the lees, and well refined,—hath a holy contempt of the baits and allurements that lie in prevailing temptations, and is safe.

(3.) He that so keeps the word of Christ's patience is always furnished with preserving considerations and preserving principles,—moral and real advantages of preservation.

1. He is furnished with preserving considerations, that powerfully influence his soul in his walking diligently with Christ. Besides the sense of duty which is always upon him, he considers,—

1st. The concernment of Christ, whom his soul loves, in him and his careful walking. He considers that the presence of Christ is with him, his eye upon him; that he ponders his heart and ways, as one greatly concerned in his deportment of himself, in a time of trial. So Christ manifests himself to do, Rev. ii. 19-23. He considers all,—

what is acceptable, what is to be rejected. He knows that Christ is concerned in his honour, that his name be not evil spoken of by reason of him; that he is concerned in love to his soul, having that design upon him to "present him holy, and unblamable, and unreprovable in his sight," Col. i. 22,—and his Spirit is grieved where he is interrupted in this work; concerned on the account of his gospel, the progress and acceptation of it in the world,—its beauty would be slurred, its good things reviled, its progress stopped, if such a one be prevailed against; concerned in his love to others, who are grievously scandalized, and perhaps ruined, by the miscarriages of such. When Hymeneus and Philetus fell, they overthrew the faith of some. And says such a soul, then, who is exercised to keep the word of Christ's patience, when intricate, perplexed, entangling temptations, public, private, personal, do arise, "Shall I now be careless? shall I be negligent? shall I comply with the world and the ways of it? Oh what thoughts of heart hath he concerning me, whose eye is upon me! Shall I contemn his honour, despise his love, trample his gospel in the mire under the feet of men, turn aside others from his ways? Shall such a man as I fly, give over resistings? It cannot be." There is no man who keeps the word of the patience of Christ but is full of this soul-pressing consideration. It dwells on his heart and spirit; and the love of Christ constrains him so to keep his heart and ways, 2 Cor. v. 14.

2dly. The great consideration of the temptations of Christ in his behalf, and the conquest he made in all assaults for his sake and his God, dwell also on his spirit. The prince of this world came upon him, every thing in earth or hell that hath either allurement or affrightment in it was proposed to him, to divert him from the work of mediation which for us he had undertaken. This whole life he calls the time of his "temptations;" but he resisted all, conquered all, and is become a Captain of salvation to them that obey him. "And," says the soul, "shall this temptation, these arguings, this plausible pretence, this sloth, this self-love, this sensuality, this bait of the world, turn me aside, prevail over me, to desert him who went before me in the ways of all temptations that his holy nature was obnoxious unto, for my good?"

3dly. Dismal thoughts of the loss of love, of the smiles of the countenance of Christ, do also frequently exercise such a soul. He knows what it is to enjoy the favour of Christ, to have a sense of his love, to be accepted in his approaches to him, to converse with him, and perhaps hath been sometimes at some loss in this thing; and so knows also what it is to be in the dark, distanced from him. See the deportment of the spouse in such a case, Cant. iii. 4. When she had once found him again, she holds him; she will not let him go; she will lose him no more.

2. He that keeps the word of Christ's patience hath preserving principles whereby he is acted. Some of them may be mentioned:—

1st. In all things he lives by faith, and is acted by it in all his ways, Gal. ii. 20. Now, upon a twofold account hath faith, when improved, the power of preservation from temptation annexed unto it:—

(1st.) Because it empties the soul of its own wisdom, understanding, and fulness, that it may act in the wisdom and fulness of Christ. The only advice for the preservation in trials and temptations lies in that of the wise man, Prov. iii. 5, "Trust in the Lord with all thine heart; and lean not unto thine own understanding." This is the work of faith; it is faith; it is to live by faith. The great [cause of] falling of men in trials is their leaning to, or leaning upon, their own understanding and counsel. What is the issue of it? Job xviii. 7, "The steps of his strength shall be straitened, and his own counsel shall cast him down." First, he shall be entangled, and then cast down; and all by his own counsel, until he come to be ashamed of it, as Ephraim was, Hos. x. 6. Whenever in our trials we consult our own understandings, hearken to self-reasonings, though they seem to be good, and tending to our preservation, yet the principle of living by faith is stifled, and we shall in the issue be cast down by own own counsels. Now, nothing can empty the heart of this self-fulness but faith, but living by it, but not living to ourselves, but having Christ live in us by our living by faith on him.

(2dly.) Faith, making the soul poor, empty, helpless, destitute in itself, engages the heart, will, and power of Jesus Christ for assistance; of which I have spoken more at large elsewhere.

2dly. Love to the saints, with care that they suffer not upon our account, is a great preserving principle in a time of temptations and trials. How powerful this was in David, he declares in that earnest prayer, Ps. lxix. 9, "Let not them that wait on thee, O Lord God of hosts, be ashamed for my sake: let not those that seek thee be confounded for my sake, O God of Israel;"—"O let not me so miscarry, that those for whom I would lay down my life should be put to shame, be evil spoken of, dishonoured, reviled, contemned on my account, for my failings." A selfish soul, whose love is turned wholly inwards, will never abide in a time of trial.

Many other considerations and principles that those who keep the word of Christ's patience, in the way and manner before described, are attended withal, might be enumerated; but I shall content myself to have pointed at these mentioned.

And will it now be easy to determine whence it is that so many in our days are prevailed on in the time of trial,—that the hour of temptation comes upon them, and bears them down more or less before it? Is it not because, amongst the great multitude of professors that we have, there are few that keep the word of the patience of Christ? If we wilfully neglect or cast away our interest in the promise of preservation, is it any wonder if we be not preserved? There is an hour of temptation come upon the world, to try them that dwell therein. It variously exerts its power and efficacy. There is not any way or thing wherein it may not be seen acting and putting forth itself. In worldliness; in sensuality; in looseness of conversation; in neglect of spiritual duties, private, public; in foolish, loose, diabolical opinions; in haughtiness and ambition; in envy and wrath; in strife and debate, revenge, selfishness; in atheism and contempt of God, doth it appear. They are but branches of the same root, bitter streams of the same fountain, cherished by peace, prosperity, security, apostasies of professors, and the like. And, alas! how many do daily fall under the power of this temptation in general! How few keep their garments girt about them, and undefiled! And if any urging, particular temptation befall any, what instances almost have we of any that escape? May we not describe our condition as the apostle that of the Corinthians, in respect of an outward visitation: "Some are sick, and some are weak, and many sleep?" Some are wounded, some defiled, many utterly lost. What is the spring and fountain of this sad condition of things? Is it not, as hath been said?—we do not keep the word of Christ's patience in universal close walking with him, and so lose the benefit of the promise given and annexed thereunto.

Should I go about to give instances of this thing, of professors coming short of keeping the word of Christ, it would be a long work. These four heads would comprise the most of them:—First, Conformity to the world, which Christ hath redeemed us from, almost in all things, with joy and delight in promiscuous compliances with the men of the world. Secondly, Neglect of duties which Christ hath enjoined, from close meditation to public ordinances. Thirdly, Strife, variance, and debate among ourselves, woful judging and despising one another, upon account of things foreign to the bond of communion that is between the saints. Fourthly, Self-fulness as to principles, and selfishness as to ends. Now, where these things are, are not men carnal? Is the word of Christ's patience effectual in them? Shall they be preserved? They shall not.

Would you, then, be preserved and kept from the hour of temptation? would you watch against entering into it?—as deductions from what hath been delivered in this chapter, take the ensuing cautions:—

1. Take heed of leaning on deceitful assistances; as,—

(1.) On your own counsels, understandings, reasonings. Though you argue in them never so plausibly in your own defence, they will leave you, betray you. When the temptation comes to any height, they will all turn about, and take part with your enemy, and plead as much for the matter of the temptation, whatever it be, as they pleaded against the end and issue of it before.

(2.) The most vigorous actings, by prayer, fasting, and other such means, against that particular lust, corruption, temptation, wherewith you are exercised and have to do. This will not avail you if, in the meantime, there be neglects on other accounts. To hear a man wrestle, cry, contend as to any particular of temptation, and immediately fall into worldly ways, worldly compliances, looseness, and negligence in other things,—it is righteous with Jesus Christ to leave such a one to the hour of temptation.

(3.) The general security of saints' perseverance and preservation from total apostasy. Every security that God gives us is good in its kind, and for the purpose for which it is given to us; but when it is given for one end, to use it for another, that is not good or profitable. To make use of the general assurance of preservation from total apostasy, to support the spirit in respect of a particular temptation, will not in the issue advantage the soul; because notwithstanding that, this or that temptation may prevail. Many relieve themselves with this, until they find themselves to be in the depth of perplexities.

2. Apply yourselves to this great preservation of faithful keeping the word of Christ's patience, in the midst of all trials and temptations:—

(1.) In particular, wisely consider wherein the word of Christ's patience is most likely to suffer in the days wherein we live and the seasons that pass over us, and so vigorously set yourselves to keep it in that particular peculiarly. You will say, "How will we know wherein the word of Christ's patience in any season is likely to suffer?" I answer, Consider what works he peculiarly performs in any season; and neglect of his word in reference to them is that wherein his word is like to suffer. The works of Christ wherein he hath been peculiarly engaged in our days and seasons seem to be these:—

1. The pouring of contempt upon the great men and great things of the world, with all the enjoyments of it. He hath discovered the nakedness of all earthly things, in overturning, overturning, overturning, both men and things, to make way for the things that cannot be shaken.

2. The owning of the lot of his own inheritance in a distinguishing manner, putting a difference between the precious and the vile, and causing his people to dwell alone, as not reckoned with the nations.

3. In being nigh to faith and prayer, honouring them above all the strength and counsels of the sons of men.

4. In recovering his ordinances and institutions from the carnal administrations that they were in bondage under by the lusts of men, bringing them forth in the beauty and the power of the Spirit.

Wherein, then, in such a season, must lie the peculiar neglect of the word of Christ's patience? Is it not in setting a value on the world and the things of it, which he hath stained and trampled under foot? Is it not in the slighting of his peculiar lot, his people, and casting them into the same considerations with the men of the world? Is it not in leaning to our own counsels and understandings? Is it not in the defilement of his ordinances, by giving the outward court of the temple to be trod upon by unsanctified persons? Let us, then, be watchful, and in these things keep the word of the patience of Christ, if we love our own preservation.

(2.) In this frame urge the Lord Jesus Christ with his blessed promises, with all the considerations that may be apt to take and hold the King in his galleries, that may work on the heart of our blessed and merciful High Priest, to give suitable succour at time of need.

Chapter 9

General exhortation to the duty prescribed.

Having thus passed through the considerations of the duty of watching that we enter not into temptation, I suppose I need not add motives to the observance of it. Those who are not moved by their own sad experiences, nor the importance of the duty, as laid down in the entrance of this discourse, must be left by me to the farther patience of God. I shall only shut up the whole with a general exhortation to them who are in any measure prepared for it by the consideration of what hath been spoken. Should you go into an hospital, and see many persons lying sick and weak, sore and wounded, with many filthy diseases and distempers, and should inquire of them how they fell into this condition, and they shall all agree to tell you such or such a thing was the occasion of it,—"By that I got my wound," says one, "And my disease," says another,—would it not make you a little careful how or what you had to do with that thing or place? Surely it would. Should you go to a dungeon, and see many miserable creatures bound in chains for an approaching day of execution, and inquire the way and means whereby they were brought into that condition, and they should all fix on one and the same thing, would you not take care to avoid it? The case is so with entering into temptation. Ah! how many poor, miserable, spiritually-wounded souls, have we everywhere!—one wounded by one sin, another by another; one falling into filthiness of the flesh, another of the spirit. Ask them, now, how they came into this estate and condition? They must all answer, "Alas! we entered into temptation, we fell into cursed snares and entanglements; and that hath brought us into the woful condition you see!" Nay, if a man could look into the dungeons of hell, and see the poor damned souls that lie bound in chains of darkness, and hear their cries, what would he be taught? What do they say? Are they not cursing their tempters, and the temptations that they entered in? And shall we be negligent in this thing? Solomon tells us that the "simple one that follows the strange woman knows not that the dead are there, that her house inclineth to death, and her paths to the dead" (which he repeats three times); and that is the reason that he ventures on her snares. If you knew what hath been done by entering into temptation, perhaps you would be more watchful and careful. Men may think that they shall do well enough notwithstanding; but, "Can a man take fire in his bosom, and his clothes not be burnt? Can one go upon hot coals, and his feet not be burnt?" Prov. vi. 27, 28. No such thing; men come not out of their temptation without wounds, burnings, and scars. I know not any place in the world where there is more need of pressing this exhortation than in this place. Go to our several colleges, inquire for such and such young men; what is the answer in respect of many? "Ah! such a one was very hopeful for a season; but he fell into ill company, and he is quite lost. Such a one had some good beginning of religion, we were in great expectation of him; but he is fallen into temptation." And so in other places. "Such a one was useful and humble, adorned the gospel; but now he is so wofully entangled with the world that he is grown all self, hath no sap nor savour. Such a one was humble and zealous; but he is advanced, and hath lost his first love and ways." Oh! how full is the world, how full is this place, of these woful examples; to say nothing of those innumerable poor creatures who are fallen into temptation by delusions in religion. And is it not time for us to awake before it be too late,—to watch against the first rising of sin, the first attempts of Satan, and all ways whereby he hath made his approaches to us, be they never so harmless in themselves?

Have we not experience of our weakness, our folly, the invincible power of temptation, when once it is gotten within us? As for this duty that I have insisted on, take these considerations:—

1. If you neglect it, it being the only means prescribed by our Saviour, you will certainly enter into temptation, and as certainly fall into sin. Flatter yourselves. Some of you are "old disciples;" have a great abhorrency of sin; you think it impossible you should ever be seduced so and so; but, "Let him (whoever he be) that thinketh he standeth take heed lest he fall." It is not any grace received, it is not any experience obtained, it is not any resolution improved, that will preserve you from any evil, unless you stand upon your watch: "What I say unto you," says Christ, "I say unto all, Watch." Perhaps you may have had some good success for a time in your careless frame; but awake, admire God's tenderness and patience, or evil lies at the door. If you will not perform this duty, whoever you are, one way or other, in one thing or other, spiritual or carnal wickedness, you will be tempted, you will be defiled; and what will be the end thereof? Remember Peter!

2. Consider that you are always under the eye of Christ, the great captain of our salvation, who hath enjoined us to watch thus, and pray that we enter not into temptation. What think you are the thoughts and what the heart of Christ, when he sees a temptation hastening towards us, a storm rising about us, and we are fast asleep? Doth it not grieve him to see us expose ourselves so to danger, after he hath given us warning upon warning? Whilst he was in the days of his flesh he considered his temptation whilst it was yet coming, and armed himself against it. "The prince of this world cometh," says he, "but hath no part in me." And shall we be negligent under his eye? Do not think that thou seest him coming to thee as he did to Peter, when he was asleep in the garden, with the same reproof: "What! canst thou not watch one hour?" Would it not be a grief to thee to be so reproved, or to hear him thundering against thy neglect from heaven, as against the church of Sardis? Rev. iii. 2.

3. Consider that if thou neglect this duty, and so fall into temptation,—which assuredly thou wilt do,—that when thou art entangled God may withal bring some heavy affliction or judgment

upon thee, which, by reason of thy entanglement, thou shalt not be able to look on any otherwise than as an evidence of his anger and hatred; and then what wilt thou do with thy temptation and affliction together? All thy bones will be broken, and thy peace and strength will be gone in a moment. This may seem but as a noise of words for the present; but if ever it be thy condition, thou wilt find it to be full of woe and bitterness. Oh! then, let us strive to keep our spirits unentangled, avoiding all appearance of evil and all ways leading thereunto; especially all ways, businesses, societies, and employments that we have already found disadvantageous to us.

Footnotes

1. Heb. ii. 9; Gal. iii. 13; 2 Cor. v. 21.
2. Gen. xxii. 1, 2.
3. Matt. iv. 8.
4. Mortification of Sin in Believers, vol. vi. chap. xiv. p. 78.